WEB DESIGN

for teens

Maneesh Sethi

COURSE TECHNOLOGY
CENGAGE Learning™

Web Design for Teens

Publisher:
Stacy L. Hiquet

Senior Marketing Manager:
Sarah O'Donnell

Marketing Manager:
Heather Hurley

Manager of Editorial Services:
Heather Talbot

Associate Acquisitions Editor:
Megan Belanger

Senior Editor:
Mark Garvey

Associate Marketing Manager:
Kristin Eisenzopf

Marketing Coordinator:
Jordan Casey

Project Editor:
Jenny Davidson

Technical Reviewer:
Jeff Belanger

PTR Editorial Services Coordinator:
Elizabeth Furbish

Copy Editor:
Sean Medlock

Teen Reviewers:
Daniel Ross Merrill
Jonathan Milton Bailey

Interior Layout Tech:
Marian Hartsough

Cover Designer:
Michael Tanamachi

Indexer:
Sharon Shock

Proofreader:
Laura Gabler

Library of Congress Catalog Card Number: 2004114412
ISBN 13: 978-1-59200-607-6
ISBN 10: 1-59200-607-8

Course Technology, a division of Cengage Learning
20 Channel Center Street
Boston, MA 02210
www.courseptr.com

Printed in Canada
5 6 7 8 9 11 10 09 08

For Nagina, Rachi, and Ramit

Acknowledgments

Wow, there are so many people to thank. This book has been an excellent project for me, and I'm really thankful for everyone who worked with me on this book.

Special thanks to Jenny Davidson, one of my editors on my book. Jenny, thanks so much for your help throughout the process (and for writing my recommendation!). Sean Medlock, Megan Belanger, and Jeff Belanger, thank you so much for working so hard on my book. Also, thanks to Emi Smith, who has helped me do my job throughout my book-writing process.

Thanks to my parents, Neelam and Prabhjot Sethi, who have helped me so much, and not only in writing the book. Thanks to my brothers and sisters, Rachita, Nagina, and Ramit, who have always been there for me. Thank you for the motivation and the help that you have given me.

Also, thanks to my friends. Shawn Gogia, Jack Reilly, and Dallin Parkinson, thank you very much for a great year. You too, Peter Stamos and Katelyn Schirmer, Kristen Dohnt, Adam Hepworth, Miles Brodsky, Mike Gertz, David Wu, Greg Imamura, Colin White, Brad Freeman, Lindsay Hoffman, Tyson Johnson, Brian Haight, Jenny Benbow, David Hine, Matt Gandley, Molly King, and everyone else who are my best friends. Let's stay in touch during college.

Don't forget my teachers. To Mr. Erickson, Ms. Nichols, Mrs. Pino-Jones, Miss Sue (Mrs. Eddington?), Mrs. Yost, Mrs. Whitford, Mr. Waugh, Mr. Webster, Mrs. Shenoy, and everyone else who has helped me throughout my high-school career; thank you so much. Shoot, and while I'm here, I might as well say thanks to Mr. Hand, even though you make fun of me way too much for my math skills.

Lastly, thank you! If it wasn't for you, this book wouldn't be possible. Hey, if you didn't buy it, I'd be out a couple of bucks anyway.

I know I forgot some people, and they're gonna be really mad that I forgot about them. That is why you can sign your name right below, and it'll be just like I put your name in here!

_____

About the Author

MANEESH SETHI attends high school in Fair Oaks, California. He will be attending college in the Fall. He has been an avid Web designer for several years. Sethi runs Standard Design, designing and developing Web sites. He is the author of *Game Programming for Teens* and *How to Succeed as a Lazy Student*. Visit his Web site at www.maneeshsethi.com or e-mail him at maneesh@maneeshsethi.com.

Contents at a Glance

Contents

Introduction

Hey, thanks for picking up this book. I really appreciate it. Seriously.

So what are you going to learn in this book? I'm going to teach you about the art of Web design. After reading these few hundred pages, you will be able to build your own Web site!

Web design is the creation of Web sites. With Web sites, you can have your own identity online, a way for you to be able to tell others about yourself. The best part is that Web sites aren't too expensive to own or make.

There are two parts to design: coding the pages and creating the design. This book teaches you both. You'll learn HTML, the language that is used to make Web sites. After that, you'll learn how to use HTML to make well-designed, appealing pages.

This book strives to teach HTML and design in easy-to-understand sections. You won't find anything too difficult here. Even though this book is called *Web Design for Teens*, that doesn't mean that only teens will benefit. People of all ages can learn Web design from this book.

What's in the Book?

This book is going to teach you everything you need to design an excellent Web site. Each chapter adds on to the previous chapter, and you will learn more and more about design as you move through the book.

Part 1 is an introduction to the book. You will learn more about what we are going to discuss and also about the individual elements of a Web page. We will also go over some basic ideas of HTML.

Part 2 teaches HTML (Hypertext Markup Language). This is the language that goes into each Web page—the code that makes the page appear on the screen. You will learn everything from basic HTML to advanced topics in this section.

Part 3 covers the design of Web sites. You will learn how to incorporate your HTML into a well-designed site. We will go over proper colors and navigation systems within your individual Web sites.

Part 4 explains how to take your Web site to the next level. You will learn how to put your Web site online, how to advertise it, and how to attract visitors.

Part 5 contains all of the appendixes. There is a glossary of the definitions and maxims used in the book, along with a list of what is on the companion Web site.

How Do I Download the Source?

There are a couple of ways you can get all of the programs and source used in the book. You can download these programs and source from my Web site, http://www.maneesh-sethi.com, or from the publisher's Web site, http://www.courseptr.com/downloads. You can also download the programs and learn more about my other projects, such as my other books *Game Programming for Teens* and *How to Succeed as a Lazy Student*, from the maneeshsethi.com Web site.

What Do I Need to Know to Understand the Book?

You don't need any previous coding knowledge to read the book. All you need is the Internet and a little bit of basic information about how to use a Web browser. If you have a Windows PC or a Macintosh, you will probably be able to run any programs in the book.

There are a few elements that I use in this book to explain items. You will find Tips, Cautions, Notes, Sidebars, Definitions, and Maxims.

Tips are little tricks that will help you enhance your Web pages.

Cautions are things that you should be careful about so that you don't make any unnecessary errors.

Notes give a greater explanation to what is going on.

SIDEBAR

Sidebars are long explanations about tricks and methods of getting something done.

 Definitions explain some term that relates to Web design.

 Maxims explain some important facet of design. These maxims are things that you should follow to design excellent Web sites.

That's it for the introduction. Feel free to e-mail me at any time at maneesh@maneeshsethi.com, and check out the book's Web site at www.maneeshsethi.com.

Thanks for buying the book!

PART 1

WEB DESIGN

Introduction to Web Design

This part introduces the basics. You will learn how to identify good and bad design as well as HTML source.

This part will guide you to a basic understanding of the Web design process. Using the information you learn from this part, you will be able to understand the more complex parts of design and HTML.

Chapter 1
Getting to Know Web Sites

Welcome to the amazing world of Web sites. As you know, the Internet is a very big thing these days, and everyone wants to have a presence on it. You may have heard of things such as Web logs (called *blogs*), e-commerce Web sites where people can buy and sell stuff, and personal sites where people just talk about themselves and things they like to do. This book is going to show you how to do all of them.

Web site design is not the easiest thing in the world, so I'm going to demonstrate how to make a Web site in the most painless way possible. Let me give you a rundown of what you'll learn in this book.

What's Coming Up?

In the first part of the book, you'll learn about the basics of a Web site. That includes this chapter, where I'll explain the background of this book and of Web site design. Also included in this part is a basic explanation of design. You should learn about design before you get into actual Web design, and this part will give you a short primer.

In Part 2, you'll learn HTML, otherwise known as *Hypertext Markup Language.* This may sound complex and a little scary, but it isn't really that bad. It's just a uniform way to make Web sites appear on the screen.

 **Definition**

HTML (Hypertext Markup Language) This is the backbone code of every Web page. It makes the text and graphics appear on the screen.

Things such as line breaks, tables, and bullet-point lists can be done easily using HTML.

Part 3 of the book talks about design issues for Web sites. One of my biggest pet peeves is visiting a Web site that's poorly designed and horrible to look at. Ugly sites make your Web experience no fun. Seriously.

The fourth and final part of the book teaches everything else. What does "everything else" consist of, you might ask. Well, Part 4 teaches how to take the Web site you've designed and put it on the Internet for everyone else to see. I'll show you some places where you can buy your own domain name, such as www.Whateveryouwant.com. For example, my site is named www.ManeeshSethi.com, and I spend only about $29 on it *per year.* Cool, eh? Check out Figure 1.1 for a picture of my site.

Anyway, that's enough of this boring intro. Let's move on to something more interesting: the program we'll be using to do our work.

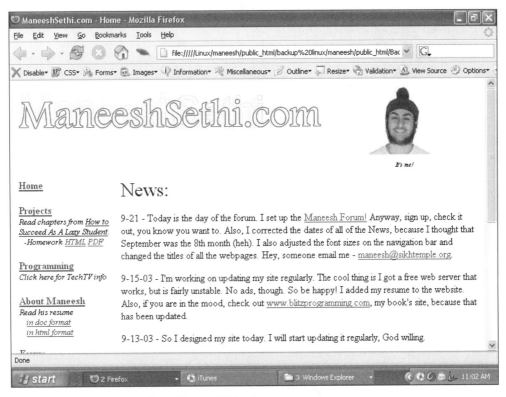

FIGURE 1.1 *The ManeeshSethi.com Web site.*

Learning About the Program: It's Nvu Time

Most of what we do will be done in pure HTML. (I'll give you an example of what an HTML Web page looks like near the end of the chapter.) However, sometimes it's nice to have a program that does a little of the work for you. This is Nvu's (pronounced n-view) job. Figure 1.2 shows you a picture of Nvu.

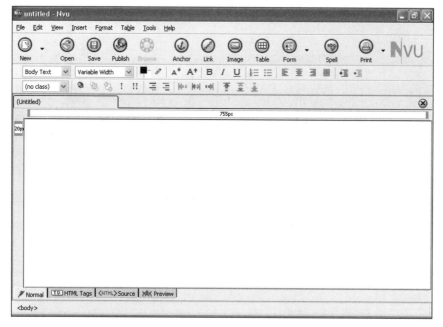

FIGURE 1.2 *The Nvu HTML editor.*

Nvu is an *open source* program. That means anyone can download and use it for free. You can find it at www.nvu.com.

Before we go any further, I want you to know where you can find all the files I refer to in the book. You can download the files from the Course Web site (www.courseptr.com/downloads). Once on the site, click the Downloads link. You can also find them on my own Web site, www.maneeshsethi.com/wdft.html. Visit the site and make sure you are in the *Web Design for Teens* section, and you can download all of the source and programs from there.

What Is Nvu?

Nvu is a program that lets you design Web sites while shielding you from the actual code. It lets you see what your Web pages will look like while you design them, rather than forcing you to check it later in a browser.

Now, what's the difference between Nvu and pure HTML? Well, pure HTML is just text. That's it. Everything you write is text. For example, let's say you want to post the following on the Web:

> Wow, Maneesh is amazing.
>
> And he's incredible, too.

Here's the HTML to make a complete Web page that says this:

```
<HTML>
<BODY>
<P>
Wow, Maneesh is amazing.
<BR>
And he's incredible, too.
</BODY>
</HTML>
```

A lot uglier than plain English, huh? You might be asking what those things in brackets are, like <HTML>. Those are just commands that make stuff appear on the screen, and you'll learn all about them in Part 2. Figure 1.3 shows how this code appears in the Web browser.

FIGURE 1.3 *How HTML code appears in the Web browser.*

Back to the point, the beautiful thing about Nvu is that it allows you to design Web sites either with or without HTML. You can type out all of your text and see what it will look like on the screen, and then you can switch to HTML and check out the actual code behind what you're doing. By looking at the code, you can do more advanced (and quicker!) editing of a Web page, and you'll have more control over what's onscreen.

Nvu is a WYSIWYG editor. Big word, huh? It stands for *What You See Is What You Get*. This means that when you're editing the document in Nvu, you see what's onscreen as you edit it. When you insert images into the WYSIWYG editor, you know exactly how they'll appear on the Web. In addition, Nvu is a pure HTML editor, so you can edit the code directly if you want.

WYSIWYG (What You See Is What You Get)

This type of editor allows you to see exactly what will appear on the screen as you edit the file.

Pure HTML Editor

This type of editor enables you to write and edit the HTML code directly.

An HTML editor is simply a text editor. Notepad, for example, is a text editor and a pure HTML editor.

Anyway, I'm sure you want to start actually doing something. Let's install the program and take a look at it.

Installing the Program: Let's Get This Party Started

I don't know if you've ever installed a program or not, but it shouldn't be too difficult. If you're not using your own computer, ask a parent for permission and whatnot.

Nvu is an HTML editor and is different from a Web browser—if you want the best Web browser that man has ever created, download Mozilla Firefox as well (www.mozilla.org). Seriously. It's absolutely awesome. We'll talk more about this later in the book.

First things first. You need to download the program. Go ahead and do so. An installation screen that looks much like the one in Figure 1.4 pops up.

Not too shabby, eh? Click Next a couple of times. If you want, you can change the directory where it's installed, but you probably don't need to.

Continue to click Next until you get to the Ready to Install screen. Then click Install and wait until it's done. As soon as it's done, open up the program you just installed. It should look a lot like Figure 1.2.

Play around with the browser if you like. Once you feel like jumping into Nvu, come back here. I'll be waiting . . .

. . . Back already? Cool, let's work on Nvu. Opening Nvu is easy—all you need to do is open it from your Applications menu. Open up the Start menu, go to All Programs, and look for Nvu, as shown in Figure 1.5.

Click the icon to open Nvu. It looks pretty complex, but I'll walk you through everything there is to know about the program. Figure 1.6 shows you what Nvu looks like.

FIGURE 1.4 *The Nvu installation screen.*

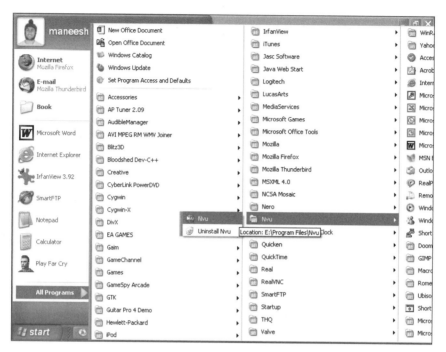

FIGURE 1.5 *Accessing Nvu from your computer.*

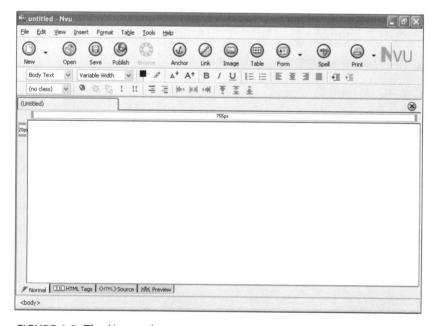

FIGURE 1.6 *The Nvu main screen.*

Understanding Nvu

Nvu can look a little daunting at first. There are a lot of icons and menus that seem vague and weird, but don't worry, you won't have to use all of them. The first thing you'll see is a blank screen and a flashing cursor, as shown in Figure 1.6.

If you ever have any problems understanding anything in Nvu, you can use the help system on the menu bar. Just go to Help > FAQ. From there, you can get all the help you need.

 note The > symbol means a selection from a menu. In other words, File > New instructs you to open the File menu and select New. The menus can be found at the top of the Nvu window, right above the main toolbar.

A lot of the menus and toolbars will be very useful for Web site design, so we should go over all of them now.

Windows and Panels

The main window takes up the most space onscreen. When you open up the window, it should be completely blank except for a flashing cursor. You can type in anything and it will appear in the main window. Figure 1.7 shows what it looks like when you type something.

Sure, you might be thinking, "Wow, that's boring. All I can see is plain ol' text." Right now, it's pretty boring. But take a look at Figure 1.8, which shows you the HTML that Nvu has saved you from having to type.

A lot easier, huh? The cool thing is that Nvu can put in images and tables and things like that, which can drastically reduce the time it takes to create a Web site. By the way, to switch from WYSIWYG mode to pure HTML mode, as I did between Figures 1.7 and 1.8, just alternate between the menu options View > Normal Edit Mode and View > HTML Source.

So that's the main window. Let's move on to the toolbars.

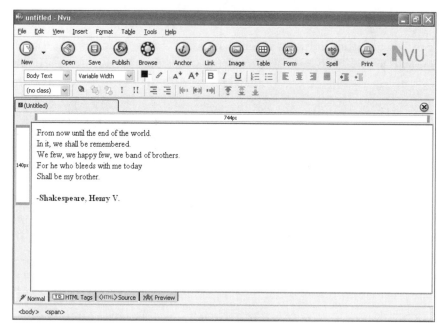

FIGURE 1.7 *Typing in Nvu, Shakespeare-style.*

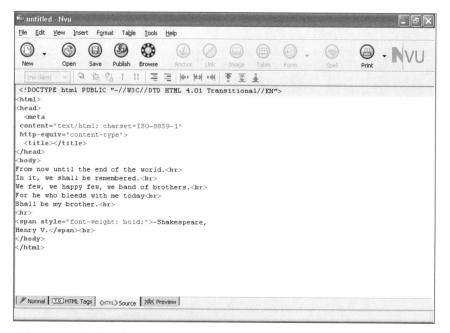

FIGURE 1.8 *Typing in Nvu, HTML-style.*

Toolbars

There are two major toolbars that we should check out. The first is the composition toolbar, shown in Figure 1.9. This toolbar makes common functions really easy to do, such as opening new documents, printing, or creating hyperlinks.

FIGURE 1.9 *Compositon toolbar.*

Not too shabby, eh? Table 1.1 gives a list of all of the icons and their functions.

TABLE 1.1 Composition Toolbar Shortcut Icons

Icon	Description
New	Creates a new blank Web page document.
Open	Opens a previously existing Web page.
Save	If your program has been saved previously, the Save icon quickly saves the open document. If not, Save asks for a filename and a location to save the file in.
Publish	Allows you to put your Web site online.
Browse	Opens up your file in a Web browser, allowing you to see what it will look like on the Web.
Anchor	Inserts a new named anchor.
Link	Inserts a new hyperlink.
Image	Inserts an image into the document.
Table	Creates a new table with a choice of the number of columns and rows.
Form	Creates a new form and different form elements.
Spell	Spellchecks the document.
Print	Prints the document.

Next up is the format toolbar, shown in Figure 1.10. Table 1.2 explains all of the icons.

FIGURE 1.10 *The format toolbar.*

TABLE 1.2 Format Toolbar Shortcut Icons

Icon	Description
Paragraph Format	Changes the size and importance of text in a document.
Color	Allows a choice of color for the font.
Highlight Color	Highlights text with an overlaid color.
Smaller/Larger Font Size	Decreases and increases the size of the text.
Bold	Makes text bold and darker.
Italicize	Italicizes text, making it stand out.
Underline	Underlines text.
Bullet/Numbered List	Creates either a bulleted or numbered list.
Align Left/Centered/Right/Justified	Aligns text in different ways on the screen.
Indent/Outdent Text	Moves text right or left. Usually used for paragraphs.

I'm sure you're getting tired of these tables of information by now, so let's take a look at a sample Web site. From there, we'll look at the HTML and talk about what it does. Let's move.

A Sample Web Site: www.ManeeshSethi.com

I'm going to show you the source code to a sample Web site so that you can see how the code works behind the scenes. For simplicity's sake, I'll use my own Web site, www.ManeeshSethi.com. Figure 1.1 showed you what the site looks like. Note that this isn't the exact source from the Web site. I have made minor changes so that it's easier to understand.

To download this source, visit www.courseptr.com/downloads and type in the title of the book, or go to www.maneeshsethi.com and go to the *Web Design for Teens* section. You will be able to download or access the source and any other programs or images from there.

Starting off at the beginning, here are the first few lines of source:

```
<html>
<head>
  <title>ManeeshSethi.com - Home</title>
</head>
```

The first thing you'll notice is that every line starts with a word surrounded by greater-than and less-than signs. Why is this? The Web browser reads any item that's within these brackets as HTML code. That is, it doesn't actually appear on the screen, but it determines how the text or images appear onscreen. The first bracketed item you see is `<html>`. This occurs at the beginning of any HTML document, and it signifies that what follows is made up of HTML.

Following that is the `<head>` `</head>` tag. This signifies the header portion of the document, which contains items that don't actually exist in the body of the

document, but are still necessary. For example, it includes the title, signified by `<title>` `</title>`, which appears at the top of the browser and in the status bar.

HTML Command
This is HTML code that's between < and > brackets. This information is read by the Web browser and influences the document, but it does not appear in the document itself.

Notice that the title is followed by `</title>`. What does this mean? It simply means that the title is over. Almost every HTML command uses an ending command that's exactly the same, except it also has a forward slash (/) before the

HTML Ending Command
This is HTML code that ends a previous command. It's signified by a backslash (/) in front of a command name, such as `</title>`.

command. (There are a few notable exceptions, but we'll get to those later.) The header ends with a `</head>` command.

```
<body>
<table style="page-break-before: always; width: 812px; height: 575px;"
 border="0" cellpadding="6" cellspacing="0">
  <col width="173"> <col width="719"> <tbody>
    <tr>
      <td colspan="2" height="91" valign="top" width="904">
      <p align="right"><img src="images/header.gif" name="Graphic1"
align="left" border="0" height="75" width="497"><img
src="images/me.jpg" name="Graphic2" align="bottom" border="0"
height="107" width="111"><br>
      <i><font size="1">It's
me!</font></i></p>
      </td>
    </tr>
```

This begins the body section of the document. I'm not going to go over all of the commands, but let me give you a quick rundown. The `<body>` command signifies that everything that follows will make up the actual document. From there, a table is created, and then a number of columns and rows. Two images are then drawn, using the `<img>` command. These two images are the ManeeshSethi.com logo and the picture of me. Lastly, the text "It's me!" is written under my picture.

```
<tr>
      <td height="437" valign="top" width="173"> <strong><a
 href="http://www.maneeshsethi.com/index.html">Home</a></strong>
<br><br>
<a href="http://www.maneeshsethi.com/books.html"><b>Projects</b></a><br>
      <i><font size="2">-Read chapters from <a href="http://www.maneesh-
sethi.com/lazystudent.html"><u>How to Succeed As A Lazy Student<br></u></a>
-Learn about <a href="http://www.maneeshsethi.com/gpft.html"><u>Game
Programming for Teens.</u></a><br>
-See my new book, <a href="http://www.maneeshsethi.com/wdft.html">Web
Design for Teens.</a><br>
<a href="lazystudent/homework.pdf"> </a></font></i>
<br><br><strong> <a
```

```
href="http://www.maneeshsethi.com/blog.html">Programming</a></strong><a
 href="file:///home/maneesh/maneeshsethi.com/programming.html"><br>
      </a> <i><font size="2">View Maneesh's Blog.<br>
      </font></i><span style="text-decoration: underline<br> </span>
<strong><a href="http://www.maneeshsethi.com/about.html">About
Maneesh</a></strong><br>
      <a href="http://www.maneeshsethi.com/forum/index.php"><b><br>
Forum</b></a></p>
    </td>
```

This section draws the navigation bar to the left. The most important thing you can find here is the command `<a href="…"> </a>`. This command creates a hyperlink that the Web site visitor can click on to go to another page. Hyperlinks are the basis of the Internet.

 Note that the links on the Web page go to the new, updated version of ManeeshSethi.com. You can access all of my new site from the links on this page. This version of the ManeeshSethi.com Web site is old, from a few years ago, but I use it here to demonstrate the basics of a Web site.

```
    <td style="width: 719px; vertical-align: top;">Welcome
to ManeeshSethi.com. Enjoy your visit here, and visit all of the links
that you can!<br>
      </td>
    </tr>
  </tbody>
</table>
<p><a href="mailto:maneesh@maneeshsethi.com">maneesh@maneeshsethi.com</a>
</p>
</body>
</html>
```

This section of the code makes up the main body of the page. This is one of the simpler sections because it relies less on tables. The beginning of this section sets up an area in which to write out the major words, and then creates a few sentences using the `<p>` command. The section then closes all of the table columns and rows started above and then links to my e-mail address, maneesh@maneeshsethi.com. (Feel free to e-mail me at any time!) The last two lines of the code close the body and HTML sections by using the </body> and </html> commands.

So that's a full Web page. The process might look difficult now, but by the end of the book, this will be a cinch. I took the time to show you this code not to discourage you, but to show you what you'll learn in only a few pages of this book.

Let's look at how you can use this code on your computer.

Viewing a Web Site

It's easy to view a Web site. All you need to do is type the filename with the proper filename extension into your Web browser, and the page will open.

What's a filename extension? Well, when you create a file on a PC running Windows, every filename has two parts: the main part and the extension. The extension is the three or four letters after the period.

Filename Extension
These are the letters that appear after the period in a filename. For most Web sites, you'll use the extension .htm or .html.

For example, if there was a file called hello.zip, zip would be the extension.

When you're creating a Web page, you want to use the filename extension .htm or .html. If you use a different extension, the file probably won't show up in the Web browser.

Here are a few examples of good filenames:

- ❖ Hi.html
- ❖ index.htm
- ❖ Y1a.html

Bad filenames would be anything that doesn't end in .html or .htm:

- ❖ hello.ht
- ❖ 131
- ❖ yo.q

See what I mean? Anyway, all you have to do to execute an HTML file is make sure that the filename extension is correct. After that, just double-click the file or open it directly from the browser, and you can view your document.

I'm going to give you a quick exercise. From the www.courseptr.com/downloads or ManeeshSethi.com Web site, get to the source from the book and navigate to the chapter01 folder. There, you'll find a file called index.txt. Rename that file to either index.html or index.htm by right-clicking on it, selecting Rename, and changing the .txt to .html or .htm. Alternatively, you can just highlight the file and press F2. Figure 1.11 shows how you can rename a file on your computer.

By doing this, you'll be able to see the old ManeeshSethi.com index page. You can also do this by going to ManeeshSethi.com, but it will look very different. I used the old design of ManeeshSethi.com in this chapter because it is simpler, but you can see the new design by following the hyperlinks or sending your browser to www.maneeshsethi.com. Also, take note that the source will be different from what was shown in this chapter.

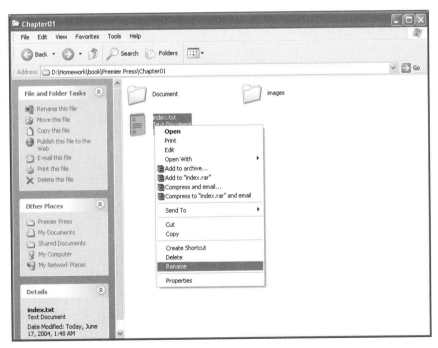

FIGURE 1.11 *Renaming a file.*

Summary

Well, now you've been introduced to Web design. You've learned what a Web site is, you've been introduced to Nvu, and you've looked at a Web page. One important thing: Do *not* be intimidated by the length or complexity of the HTML I showed you in this chapter. By the end of the book, what you've seen here will be a piece of cake.

This chapter went over the following concepts:

❖ Installing and using Nvu

❖ The major toolbars and menus in Nvu

❖ Creating your first HTML document

❖ Executing and viewing your first HTML document

I hope you enjoyed this chapter. Next up is a short discussion on design. Come back when you're ready, you hear?

Chapter 2

Welcome to Design

Hey, welcome back to the book. In this chapter, you'll learn a little bit about Web page design. In your Web-surfing, you may have noticed that some sites are easy to use and others aren't. Well, this chapter will teach you how to make your Web site one of the easier ones to use.

You might have noticed in the Table of Contents that there are four full chapters devoted to design later in this book. The difference is that this chapter is a lot more general. The later chapters will be more specific about the subjects that they teach, but this one will show everything from a high-level perspective.

The main function of this chapter is to recognize the difference between good design and bad design. Why am I explaining this so early in the book? Well, if you know what good design is, you're more likely to follow it from the beginning. This means that when you learn HTML and go about creating your own Web sites in the next part of the book, you'll already have a good foundation in design. This will help you make your Web sites as good as possible.

What are we waiting for? Let's start off by defining the word "design."

What Is Design?

"Design" is a tough word to define. What is good design? What is bad design? What is design at all? Well, Dictionary.com says that design is "the purposeful or inventive arrangement of parts or details." What does this mean to you? Probably nothing, and this just goes to show you that design is extremely hard to put a finger on.

Basically, design just means how a page looks. The organization, the ease of navigation, the number of words, and everything else on the page just contribute to the overall design. A well-designed Web page is one that is easy to look at and doesn't bother the viewer.

This explanation is boring you, right? Let me show you a couple of Web sites with good design.

First up is the perennial favorite Google.com (see Figure 2.1). Google is one of the best search engines out there, and one of the reasons for its success has been its simple and easy to use design.

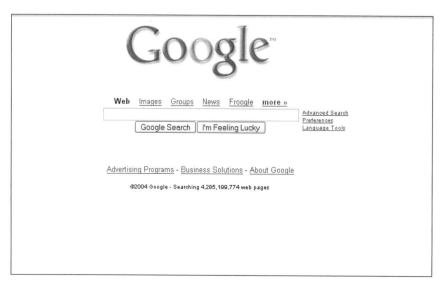

FIGURE 2.1 *The Google.com home page.*

See how easy to read everything is? In less than fifty words, the Google home page shows you exactly what it does and lets you use its services. The fonts are extremely clear and easy to read, and the colors and organization direct your eyes to the search-word text box.

Another example of good design is the Stanford University home page at www.stanford.edu. Check it out in Figure 2.2.

(By the way, if anyone asks, the reason I'm using Stanford's page as an example of good design is *not* because I'm going to apply to that college in the fall. Wink, wink.)

Stanford's Web site is awesome. The black, white, and red color scheme is extremely easy to look at, and the contrast between the font and the background makes the text stand out. Also, it's easy to understand the purpose of every part of the page.

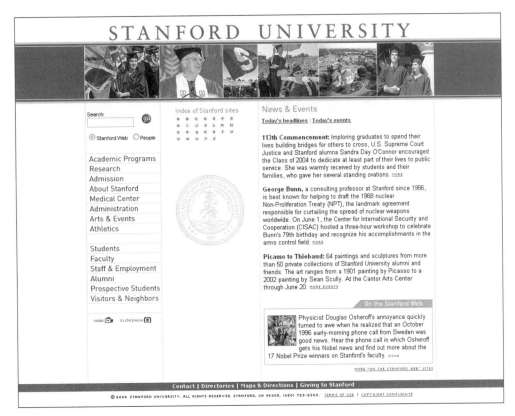

FIGURE 2.2 *The Stanford.edu home page.*

Stanford's choice of colors also reflects the school's colors, which are red and black. This Web site is a continuation of the school's look and feel.

Now, why are these two Web sites examples of good design? Because the organization of each page is so simple that it doesn't conflict with the main idea at all. This brings us to the first maxim of Web site design: *The best design is one that the user doesn't even notice.*

What this means is that a design should never prevent or hinder the user from doing what he wants to. Let's take a look at some poorly designed Web sites that fail this test. (Special thanks to webpagesthatsuck.com for these badly designed sites.)

Maxim #1
"The best design is one that the user doesn't even notice."

First up is www.homestudio.com. I believe that this is the worst-designed Web site I have ever seen. Seriously. Figure 2.3 shows you one of the pages on the site.

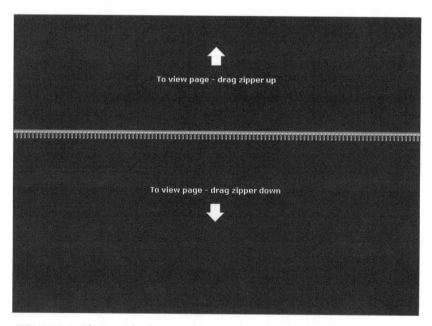

To view page - drag zipper up

To view page - drag zipper down

FIGURE 2.3 *The poorly designed Homestudio.com Web site.*

Look at this page for a second. Just look. It actually requires you to pull up a tab and pull down another tab in order to get to the Web site. *What?*

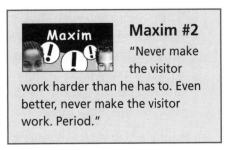

Maxim #2
"Never make the visitor work harder than he has to. Even better, never make the visitor work. Period."

This Web site is an extreme example of design gone wrong. Fortunately, sites like these allow others to learn from their mistakes and also inspire clever maxims.

All I'm trying to say is that a Web site must be easily accessible and very easy to use. Homestudio.com doesn't cut it. No one wants to spend more time than they have to wading through boring, unnecessary, useless labor.

Let's look at another example of poor design. This one isn't as bad as Homesite, but it could be a heck of a lot better. Figure 2.4 shows you http://poynterextra.org/cp/colorproject/color.html.

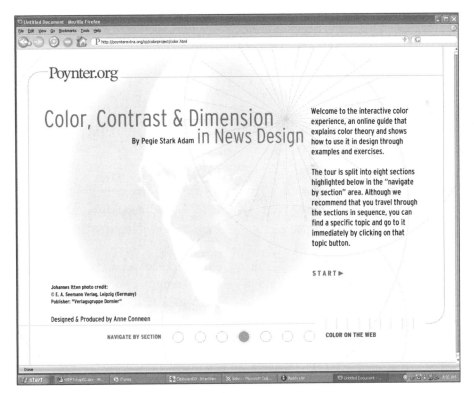

FIGURE 2.4 *The poorly designed Poynterextra.org Web site.*

This screenshot might not make it look so bad, but I invite you to visit the site. The first horrible thing you see is an overly complex Flash animation. Flash is a program that displays animation over the Internet. Sometimes it can be used well, but other times it's used too much. On this Web site, Flash is used *way* too much. The animation on the opening page takes almost 10 seconds, which is cool the first time but gets annoying after that.

Using Flash makes a page more complex than it needs to be. This leads us to our third maxim.

This maxim, or KISS for short, means that the more complex a page is, the less useable it is.

Maxim #3
"Keep it Simple, Stupid."

That isn't the end of it, though. Take a look at Figure 2.4. How are you supposed to navigate through the Web site? How do you go from one page to another? Can you figure it out?

The secret is the terribly designed navigation scheme at the bottom of the page. Figure 2.5 shows this.

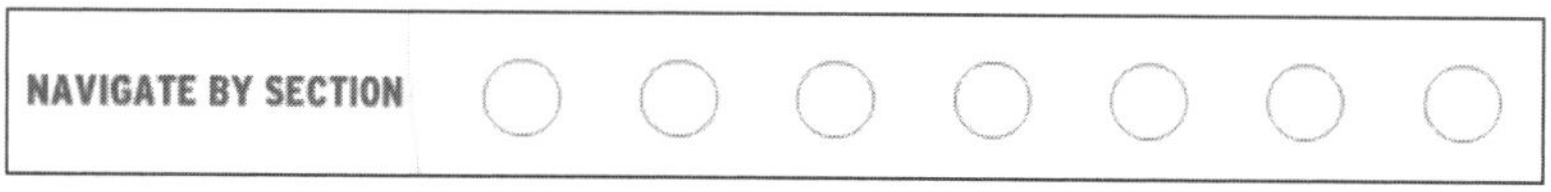

NAVIGATE BY SECTION ○ ○ ○ ○ ○ ○ ○

FIGURE 2.5 *A bad navigation scheme.*

Look at that. The navigation scheme is a bunch of empty circles! Can you tell what they mean? This is called Mystery Meat Navigation by webpagesthatsuck.com. Figure 2.6 shows what the user has to do to figure out the navigation system.

Mystery Meat Navigation

Definition This is when a user has to do extra work to find out where the navigation menu will take him.

| NAVIGATE BY SECTION   ○ ● ○ ○ ○ ○ ○   THE PHYSIOLOGY & THEORY OF COLOR |

FIGURE 2.6 *Mystery Meat Navigation.*

The visitor has to move the mouse over the navigation menu and then look off to the side of the page to find out where to go. This leads us to our fourth design maxim.

Maxim #4
"Never, ever use Mystery Meat Navigation."

Why Use Good Design?

You might wonder why all this design talk matters at all. If somebody visits a Web site and sees horrible design, a bad navigation system, and boring organization, that visitor will leave. Forever. And as a Web designer, that's the last thing you want to happen.

How can you recognize a Web site with good design? All you have to do is visit it. If you want to stay there, it's good design. If there are bright, annoying colors, the text is hard to read, or you get lost, it's bad design.

Good design is incredibly tough. Part 3 will go over mastering good design, but let me give you a quick rundown right now.

You must design your Web site before creating it. All it takes to design a site is a piece of paper and a pencil. You'll learn some design tactics in Part 3, but just remember that you need to *have* a plan before you can *follow* it.

Design should never annoy the user. That means colors, navigation schemes, and organization should all make the experience easier.

Summary

This chapter introduced you to Web site design. You now have a solid foundation that you can build on throughout the book. Remember the maxims that you've learned in this chapter when you start to design your own Web sites.

In this chapter, you learned the following:

- ❖ The definition of design
- ❖ What constitutes good design
- ❖ What constitutes bad design
- ❖ Why design makes a difference

Cool? Remember, you'll learn a lot more about design in Part 3. But next we'll look at what goes into Web sites.

Adios for now.

Chapter 3

What's in a Web Site?

This chapter will show you what's inside a Web site. Sure, you know all about design and how sites look, but this chapter will show you what goes on behind the scenes. This chapter will discuss HTML source and what sorts of elements go into Web sites, such as forms, text boxes, and lists. It will also go over some basic pre-HTML material that you should know before you advance. This chapter, along with the previous chapter on design, lays down the foundation for the rest of the book.

Get ready for the good news: In this chapter, you'll learn how to build your very own Web page! Granted, it will be extremely simple, but it'll be a real Web site nevertheless. Not bad for only the third chapter, huh?

Let's look at our first topic: The elements of a Web page.

Use the Source, Luke . . .

Let's take a moment to view the inner workings of a Web site. Following this method will allow you to read the HTML source of a page. Then, the next time you see something you like on a Web page, you can look at the HTML source and learn how to do the same thing on your own page. Don't worry, this isn't too hard to do.

First of all, open the browser of your choice. I recommend Mozilla Firefox (you can download it at www.mozilla.org), but you're probably using Internet Explorer. The following are instructions for viewing the source in Internet Explorer.

First of all, open up the browser. If you have Windows XP, the easiest way to open it is from the Start menu. See Figure 3.1.

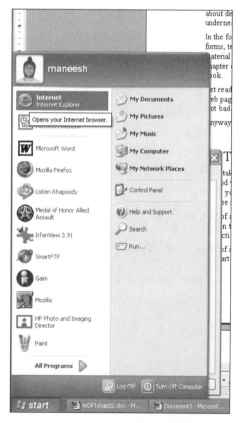

FIGURE 3.1 *Opening Internet Explorer.*

From there, go to a Web site that you enjoy. Or you can go to the best Web site ever, www.maneeshsethi.com.

Click on the View menu at the top and then select Source, as shown in Figure 3.2. The window that pops up is similar to the one in Figure 3.3.

That's a lot of words, huh? Look closely, and you'll notice that it's extremely similar to the source from the first chapter of this book.

So that's how you look at the source of a page. Try it out on a few other Web sites. It should work for all of them.

Now that you know what source *is*, let's find out what it *means*. HTML is a language that's used to describe what will be displayed onscreen. The HTML itself isn't actually shown onscreen, but talks to the computer behind the scenes. The computer changes the HTML into human language and images, and displays it on the screen.

FIGURE 3.2 *Checking the source.*

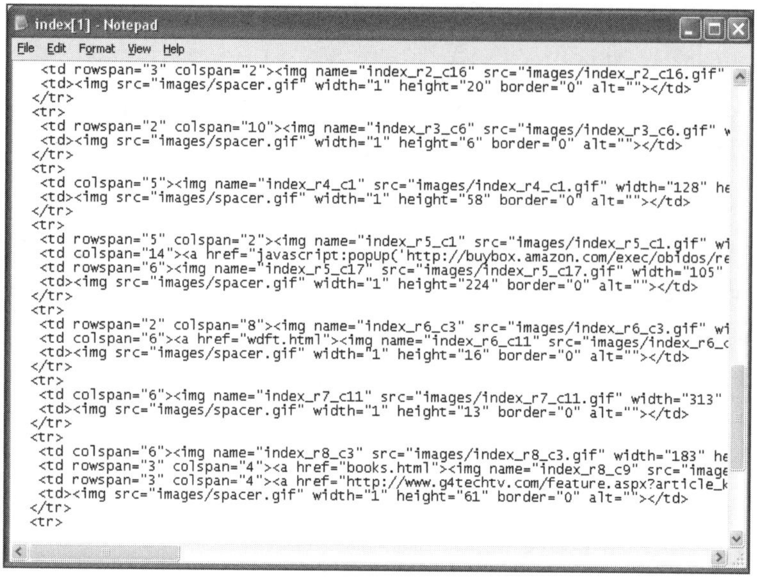

FIGURE 3.3 *The www.maneeshsethi.com source.*

In these cases, the Web browser does all the work. Internet Explorer and Firefox are the two most common browsers, and their job is to read the HTML from Web sites, interpret it, and post the results onscreen. When you select View > Source, you're seeing the actual HTML code before it's interpreted by the Web browser.

Okay, so now you have a little insight into what HTML is and how a Web browser reads it. Now let's learn about what sorts of things HTML can do.

The Elements

A Web page is made of many different parts, connected and organized into a complete product that the visitor can browse through. Let's check out these parts.

The Header

The first major part of a Web page is the header. Although the header is important, it has little actual presence on the page. It consists of the title of the page, shown in the bar at the top of the browser and in the icon in the Windows task bar. Figures 3.4 and 3.5 show what the header looks like.

FIGURE 3.4 *The header in the title bar.*

FIGURE 3.5 *The header in the task bar.*

Header information is very important to the indexing of your page on Google and other search engines. If the title of your page relates to what is searched, you have a better chance of appearing high on these search engines.

Well, that's the main part of the header. The other things that go into the header are a lot less important and obvious, and we'll discuss them later. Let's move on to the elements within the body.

The Body

The body is the main part of the HTML document. Within the body, everything that appears on the screen can be found. The first elements we'll discuss are headings.

Headings

Headings emphasize things. That's their job. You can see this by looking at the headings in this chapter. Look at the preceding header. Now compare its size to the previous header, "The Body." The same goes for headings in Web pages.

There are six different sizes of headings in HTML, and the lower the number, the bigger the heading. For example, heading 1 is much larger than heading 5. Figure 3.6 shows all of the headings in HTML, and listing WDFT03-01.html on the companion Web site (www.courseptr.com/downloads) shows the code. (I'm trying to stay away from showing you too much code, so WDFT03-01.html is found only on the Web site, instead of being copied into the book.)

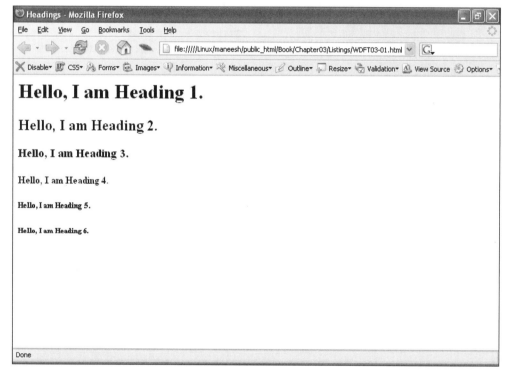

FIGURE 3.6 *The six types of headings.*

These headings serve an important function in a Web site by breaking up the text. Without headings, Web pages would be extremely wordy and boring. Headings help the reader to concentrate on what he's reading. For example, take a look at Figure 3.7, which shows text that isn't broken up by headings.

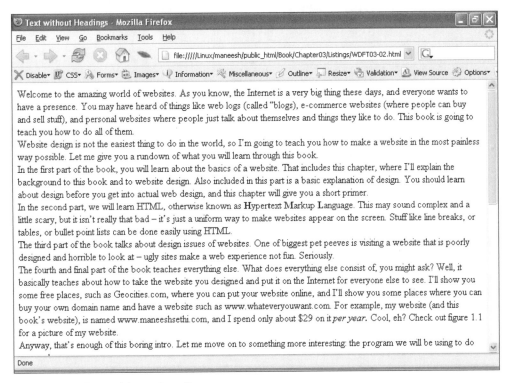

FIGURE 3.7 *Text without headings.*

See how hard that is to read? It's just . . . text. And because it's all the same size and font, nothing stands out. It's boring.

Now take a look at Figure 3.8, which is the same as Figure 3.7 but with headers.

FIGURE 3.8 *The same text with headings.*

Wow! Look at the difference. Because the text is broken up into smaller pieces, it's much easier to read and digest. I guarantee it will keep the viewer more interested as well.

Now let's move on to the next element: lists.

Lists

You don't see many lists on the Internet anymore, because they don't always fit in with a Web site. However, HTML has a feature for lists, which is awesome because it makes them extremely easy to use.

There are two main types of lists: bulleted lists and numbered lists. You've probably seen these two types of lists, but I'll refresh your memory. The following is a numbered list:

1. Hello
2. You
3. Should
4. Do
5. Something
6. Today!

Not too bad, huh? A bulleted list is a little different:

❖ The greatest trick
❖ The devil ever pulled
❖ Was convincing the world
❖ That he didn't exist

See the difference? In general, you use a numbered list when you want the viewer to follow instructions, or when you want to explain something that steps in a specific order. In contrast, a bulleted list is used to summarize information and give some explanations. Figure 3.9 shows the difference between a bulleted list and a numbered list. This Web page is WDFT03-04.html on the companion Web site.

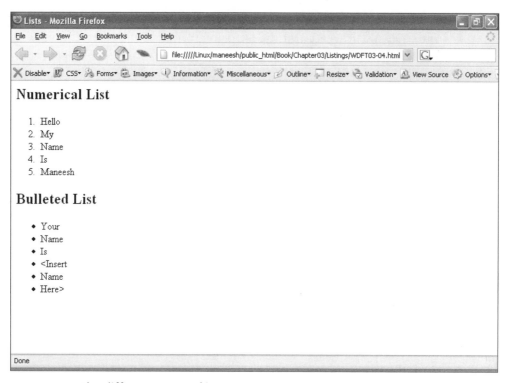

FIGURE 3.9 *The different types of lists.*

Pretty basic, eh? These lists are great for summarizing information on a Web page, because they direct the reader's focus towards the important points. Use them sparingly, though, because overuse makes them look bad.

By the way, there's one more type of list called a definition list. Figure 3.10 shows what definition lists look like, as listed in WDFT03-05.html on the companion Web site.

Definition lists are best used for explaining definitions. Use them when you're defining words within your document.

Okay, that's all for lists. Next up, we'll learn about forms.

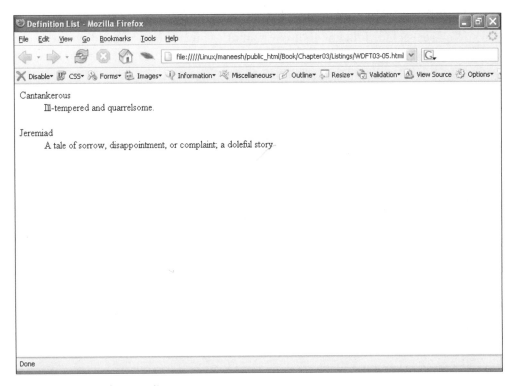

FIGURE 3.10 *Definition lists.*

Forms

The form is one of the most common elements within a Web page. Forms allow visitors to send information to the site, and they also allow e-mails to be sent from within the form. You've probably seen forms before, because they're very common on Web sites.

Forms are made up of a number of sub-elements: buttons, radio buttons, text boxes, image buttons, password boxes, check boxes, and file forms. These elements can create a form that does anything the Web designer wants.

A form usually uses all of these elements in conjunction. Using only one of these form elements does very little. In fact, at least two of them are needed for the form to do much of anything at all.

The major job of forms is to allow the visitor to send information back to the Web server. This means that you can ask your visitors to send comments to you through the site.

Figure 3.11 shows what a comment form on a Web site usually looks like.

This file is WDFT03-06.html on the companion Web site, but it won't do anything if you click Submit Query. A form has to be attached to a certain kind of document, sometimes called a CGI script, before it can send out information, and this one isn't attached to anything.

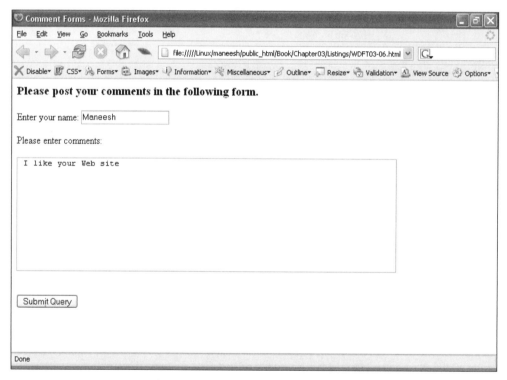

FIGURE 3.11 *A comment form.*

Comment forms aren't the only types of forms used on Web pages. Often, check boxes or drop-down lists are used. Figure 3.12 shows radio buttons, check boxes, and drop-down lists. (This file is WDFT03-07.html on the companion Web site.)

These elements work together to create a complete form. The visitor can use these elements to send information to the owner of the Web site. Using these forms, you can receive comments and ideas from your audience.

Other elements can be used to make forms work in different ways. For example, visitors can send files from their computer to your site through a form. Forms can allow people to type in passwords.

There's one more major element that we'll go over in this chapter: tables.

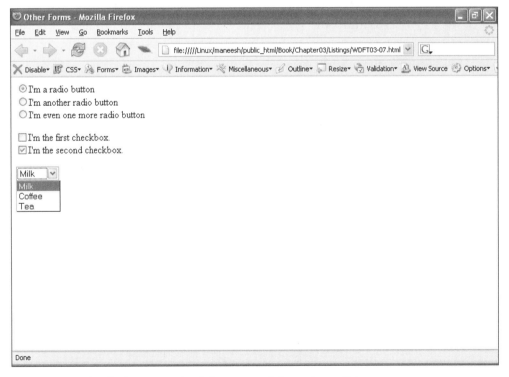

FIGURE 3.12 *Radio buttons, check boxes, and drop-down lists.*

Tables

Tables enable you to place data on a Web site, setting it off into columns and rows. Look at Table 3.1 to see what a table looks like and what it does.

Table 3.1 A Sample Table

Column#1	Column#2
I am the first row	I am the first row also, but the second column
I am the second row, first column	I am the second row, second column

You've seen tables before. They're extremely important in Web design.

In addition to simply displaying data in an organized format, invisible tables are used all over Web sites. These hidden tables allow you to organize a page so that data can be moved around on it. For example, take the old design of www.maneeshsethi.com. See how the navigation bar is on the left and the text is in the center, as shown in Figure 3.13? (This is WDFT03-08.html on the companion Web site.)

FIGURE 3.13 *Maneeshsethi.com with tables.*

Well, tables make the organization scheme work in the document. Let's try taking out all of the tables, as shown in Figure 3.14. (This is WDFT03-09.html on the companion Web site.)

Look at the difference! The first page is organized so that the navigation bar is to the left while the main section is in the center. But on the second page, without tables, there's no organization. Everything is just dumped onto the page.

Invisible tables play a huge part in developing a good-looking Web site. Organization makes a big difference in the aesthetics of a page, and tables make the page look good and function well. For this reason, invisible tables are used on almost all Web sites.

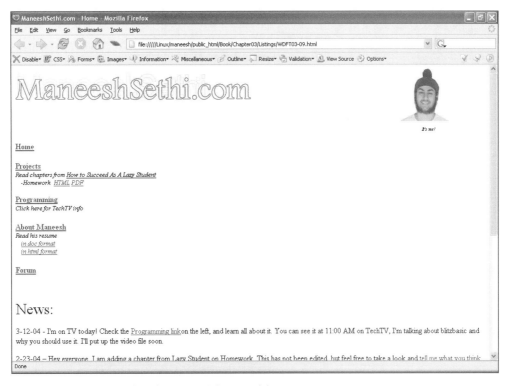

FIGURE 3.14 *Maneeshsethi.com without tables.*

Visible tables are important also. These tables allow you to organize information in an easy-to-understand format. Take a look at Figure 3.15 to see what visible tables can do. (This is WDFT03-10.html on the companion Web site.)

See? You can organize data very easily with visible tables. You can also customize the thickness of the borders to make the table look how you want.

For now, that's pretty much all you need to know about tables and the elements of the body. We'll go over each of these elements in much more depth in Part 2. Finally, to complete this chapter, we're going to make our first actual HTML document!

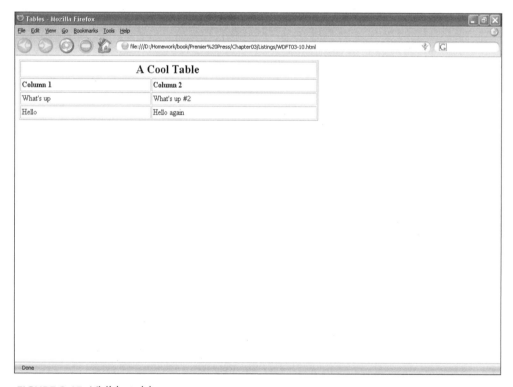

FIGURE 3.15 *Visible tables.*

Our First Page

You guys ready for the finale of this chapter? We're going to build our very own Web page. It's going to be very simple, mind you, but you'll see how easy it really is to build a page. We'll expand on these concepts as we move into the next part, on HTML.

To build a Web page using pure HTML, first you need to open up a text document. Usually, I write the code in Nvu, but for this exercise, we're going to type it directly into Notepad, the simple text editor that comes with Windows.

First, open up Notepad. The easiest method is to go to your Start menu, select Run, and type in "notepad" (see Figure 3.16).

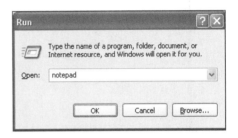

FIGURE 3.16 *Opening Notepad.*

If typing in "notepad" doesn't work, try typing in "notepad.exe" or "C:\Windows\notepad.exe".

Now that you have Notepad open, it's time to type in the HTML. Remember in the first chapter, where I talked about the intro to any HTML program? That's right, first you need to type in the following tag:

```
<HTML>
```

What does this mean? It tells the Web browser that the document is a Web page and should be drawn as such.

> **Tag—<HTML> </HTML>**
> This tag encloses the entire HTML portion of your Web page. In most cases, this is the first tag in the source.

> **tip** Whenever you code an opening tag, such as <HTML>, make sure you immediately write the closing tag, </HTML>. You won't forget if you close it immediately. First write both the opening and closing tags, and *then* write the rest of the code between the two tags.

Your Notepad window should look a lot like Figure 3.17.

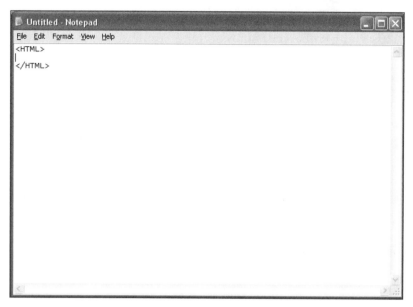

FIGURE 3.17 *The Notepad window.*

So what now? You have to create something that will appear on the screen. Let's start off with a title.

To create a title, you need to use the ‹HEAD› tag. From there, it's pretty easy to create the title. First things first. Within the two HTML tags in your Notepad window, type ‹HEAD› and ‹/HEAD› so that your document looks like this:

```
<HTML>
<HEAD>
</HEAD>
</HTML>
```

> **Tag—‹HEAD› ‹/HEAD›**
> This tag contains information that's embedded in the page but doesn't actually appear onscreen. The most important item in the header is the title, which appears on the browser icon.

HTML tags are *not* case sensitive. The Web browser reads capital letters and lowercase letters the same, as long as they're with the < and > tags. So it doesn't matter if you write <HTML></HTML> or <html></html>. Typically, I use all caps when I write my own HTML, but Nvu uses lowercase tags. Either way, it doesn't really matter. Just make sure you stick to whichever format you choose.

Within the ⟨HEAD⟩ tags, you need to write the title between a ⟨TITLE⟩ tag and a ⟨/TITLE⟩ tag. Feel free to use any title you want, but for this book, I'm going to use the title "My First Web Site." Figure 3.18 shows you what Notepad should look like at this point.

Tag—⟨TITLE⟩ ⟨/TITLE⟩

This tag defines the title of the page and places it at the top of the screen and in the system task bar.

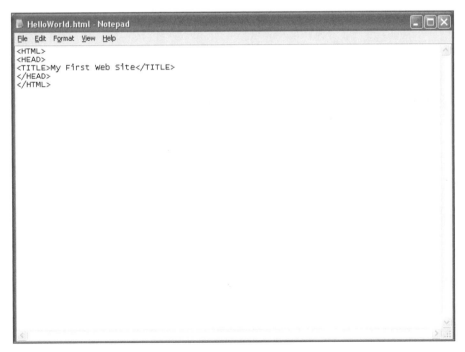

FIGURE 3.18 *The updated Notepad window.*

So now you have a title for the page. Before we learn how to open up this document and see the Web page, first let's write something in the document. After the </HEAD> tag, add the following:

```
<BODY>
Hello, World!
</BODY>
```

Now we have some actual text up in here. Let's open this up and see it in the Web browser!

> **Tag—<BODY> </BODY>**
> This tag encloses all of the text and code that actually appears on the screen.

First, save the file. In Notepad, go to File > Save and choose a location to save it in (I recommend the Desktop). Before you click Save, you need to rename the file. Change the filename to Helloworld.html. Make sure you append the .html suffix. The Save As dialog box should look something like Figure 3.19.

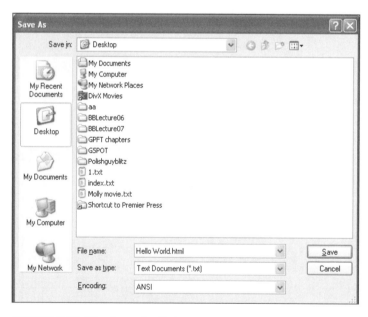

FIGURE 3.19 *The Save As dialog.*

Now that the file is saved, navigate to the folder where you saved the file. Just double-click the file, and it should open up in Internet Explorer.

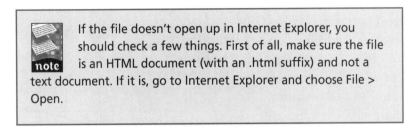 If the file doesn't open up in Internet Explorer, you should check a few things. First of all, make sure the file is an HTML document (with an .html suffix) and not a text document. If it is, go to Internet Explorer and choose File > Open.

This is your very first Web page! Figure 3.20 shows you what it should look like.

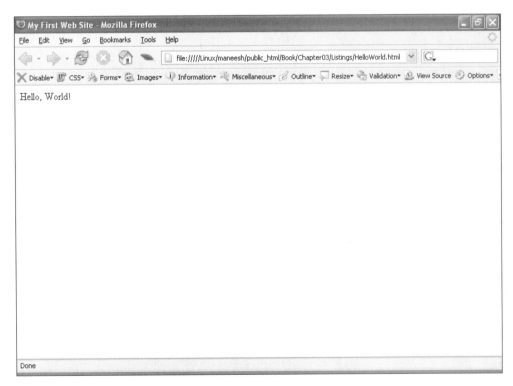

FIGURE 3.20 *The Hello World HTML file.*

Now, this is a little boring. Let's add a little bit of color. How about changing the text to white and the background to black? To do this, we need to edit the document.

Changing the color of the background involves adding an attribute to the <BODY> tag. What's an attribute? Basically, it's a command placed within a tag that changes something in

Tag Attribute

This is an addition to an HTML tag that changes the action of the tag in some way.

the document. When we add color to the document, we need to add an attribute that tells the Web browser what the color will be.

This attribute is called BGCOLOR, and it goes inside the <BODY> tag. Modify the tag in the Notepad document to look like this:

```
<BODY BGCOLOR=black>
```

Not too bad, eh? Now save it and reopen the file in the Web browser.

Uh-oh! The entire page is black. You can't see the text at all. This is because both the text and the background are black. Let's change this.

We need to add another tag, the <FONT> tag, to change the color of the text. In addition, we need to use the COLOR attribute to change the color of the text. Change the Hello, World! line to look like this:

```
<FONT COLOR=white>Hello, World!</FONT>
```

Now save the file and reopen it in the Web browser. It should look something like Figure 3.21.

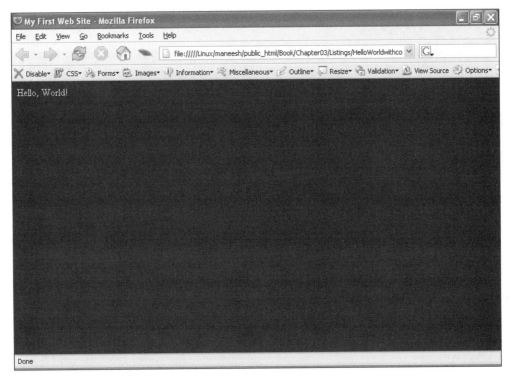

FIGURE 3.21 *The Hello World HTML file.*

All right! Your first HTML document!

That's it for our first lesson. In the coming chapters, you'll learn a lot more about using HTML to make a Web page. Things will become a lot more complex than this, but don't worry. It won't be too hard.

Summary

That's it for Part 1. In this chapter, I covered the inner workings of a Web site, including how to check its source. Everything in this chapter was very important, because it will be used throughout the book.

In this chapter, you learned the following:

❖ How to check the source of a Web page

❖ Which elements go into a Web page

❖ How to create your very own Web page

In Part 2, you'll learn some more complex HTML, and you'll practice using it in a pure HTML editor and in Nvu, a WYSIWYG editor. I hope you're ready!

PART 2

WEB
DESIGN

for
teens

Coding in HTML

Part 2 is your introduction to HTML. Throughout this part, you will learn about the foundations of the coding language and how the Web browser uses this information to display your Web page on the screen. We will go over the creation of each of the elements of Web pages, as well as how they can be used within your site.

We will also delve into the use of WYSIWYG (What You See Is What You Get) HTML editors such as Nvu, and you will learn how direct coding and these editors can work together to make excellent Web sites. We will also go over the use of style sheets, the new designing tool on the Internet.

Chapter 4

Getting Comfortable with HTML

Welcome to Part 2! In this part, you're going to learn all about HTML and Nvu. The concepts that you'll learn in Part 2 are going to be a little vague and generalized, but they will all come together in Part 3.

This chapter will introduce you to HTML. You already know a little about it, but I'm going to give you a greater knowledge of the basic concepts. I'll go into a more in-depth description of common HTML tags that you'll use, and I'll explain how to format your HTML so it's easy to read and understand.

I'll end the chapter with a quick tour of Nvu. I want to show you the power of WYSIWYG editors and how you can use them to simplify a lot of your coding. Cool?

We've got a lot of work to do, so let's get started.

Basics of HTML . . . Again

Before we move on to the new stuff, let's quickly summarize what you know about HTML. First of all, you know that it involves tags.

Tags are made up of code enclosed in angle brackets, ⟨ and ⟩. The commands inside the brackets aren't shown on the screen but are interpreted by the Web browser to change something on the screen. They put an image onscreen, or they change the font or color of the text. Many tags do things that are much more important, though, and we'll be going over these tags throughout Part 2.

First of all, you know about a few of the major tags. The first of these is ⟨HTML⟩, which is used in every Web page. It simply tells the browser that the page is going to be written in HTML. This usually goes at the beginning of the document, and the ⟨/HTML⟩ closing tag goes at the end. The next major tag is ⟨HEAD⟩, which contains information about the page but doesn't actually write anything on the screen. The most common tag used inside the ⟨HEAD⟩ tag is the ⟨TITLE⟩ tag, which defines the title of the page. The last tag that we need to go over again is the ⟨BODY⟩ tag, which tells the Web browser what will be displayed onscreen.

These three tags, ⟨HTML⟩, ⟨HEAD⟩, and ⟨BODY⟩, will appear in every Web page you design. These are the three most important tags because they're necessary for the Web page to be accessible.

Now that you know about these tags, let's find out what you can do with them. You've already learned about the header, so it's time to move to the body.

The Body

Remember the body? It's the most important part of the document, the part where everything you see appears onscreen. You need to fill the body with some text and graphics and make it look pretty. Figure 4.1 shows what the body looks like within the browser.

The body is the section of the page that's under the bookmark toolbar at the top (where it says Firefox Help) and above the status bar at the bottom. As you can see, it's pretty much the entire page.

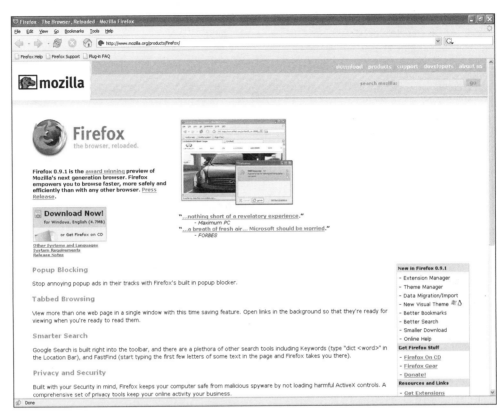

FIGURE 4.1 *The body of a document.*

Let's start off with the body's attributes. You may remember one attribute that we used in the last chapter, the BGCOLOR attribute. This allows you to define the background color of the document.

The first attribute we'll discuss is the TEXT attribute, which allows you to change the default color of all the text on a page. Remember adding a COLOR attribute to the <FONT> tag in Chapter 3, "What's in a Web Site?" That was used to change the color of the font. Adding the TEXT attribute to the <BODY> tag changes the default color for *all* text on the page.

When you change the default color of the text, you don't have to use the <FONT> tag for each block of text. It's nice to have this attribute when you have a different-color background, because if you're using a black background, you probably want all the text to be white.

How do you use this attribute? Instead of having this in your HTML source:

```
<BODY>
Insert whatever text here
</BODY>
```

you change the code to read like this:

```
<BODY COLOR=whatevercolor>
Insert whatever text here
</BODY>
```

The italicized text should be changed to fit your page. Figure 4.2 shows how the font changes in the document. (This is WDFT04-01.html on the companion Web site.)

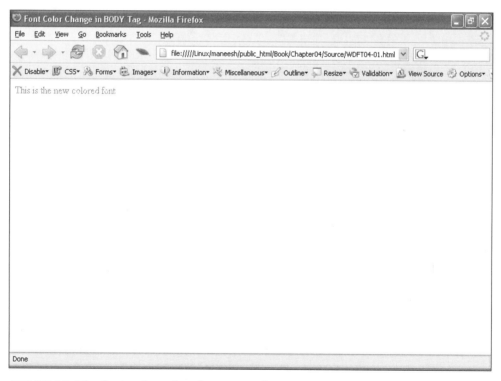

FIGURE 4.2 *The font color using the TEXT attribute.*

In Figure 4.2, the text is gray. To do this, I once again used the BODY attribute. The following is the entire text of WDFT04-01.html:

```
<HTML>

<HEAD>
<TITLE>Font Color Change in BODY Tag</TITLE>
</HEAD>

<BODY TEXT=gray>
This is the new colored font
</BODY>

</HTML>
```

By now, you might be wondering how many colors you can use on your page. Well, good news! There are a lot of them.

In Web design, there are 216 safe colors. "Safe" means that you can use these colors without having to worry about them not appearing on someone's computer because of their color count. However, not all of these colors have names like "gray" or "red."

Because you might want to use some other colors that don't have names, you might have to use hexadecimal notation. Hexadecimal is a bit hard to comprehend. It's a numbering system based on sixteen digits.

Hexadecimal Notation

Definition This is a way to define colors so that they can appear on the screen as a background or a font.

Base 10, our common numbering system, has a total of ten digits: 0, 1, 2, 3, 4, 5, 6, 7, 8, 9. In hexadecimal, there are sixteen: 0, 1, 2, 3, 4, 5, 6, 7, 8, 9, A, B, C, D, E, F. That's right, it uses letters.

None of this is a big deal. To choose the color you want, you simply pick the hexadecimal code for the appropriate color. How do you get this number, though?

The easiest way is to use a list on a Web site. One of the best lists out there is www.w3schools.com/html/html_colors.asp, shown in Figure 4.3. This shows all of the colors in a very easy-to-use format.

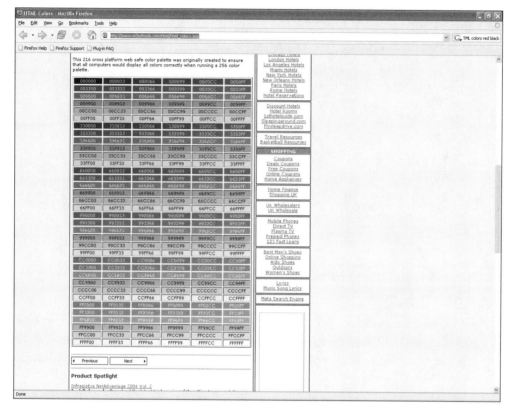

FIGURE 4.3 *The 216 safe colors.*

Even though this figure is in grayscale, you can see how each color differs from the others slightly. When you visit the page on the Web, you can see all of the different colors as they actually appear on the screen.

Notice how each color is made up of six digits. These digits include all of the hexadecimal numbers, 0-9 and A-F, and work together to create all of the colors you'll ever need.

You might be wondering how to use this on your page. The format is very similar to how we changed the color before:

1. Go to www.w3schools.com/html/html_colors.asp and pick out a color you'd like to use.

2. Note the six-digit hexadecimal code for the color you want to use.

3. Decide whether the color will be used for font color or background color.

4. Inside the BODY tag, choose the appropriate attribute and add =#*xxxxxx*.

What does #*xxxxxx* mean? Replace the *x*'s with the hexadecimal code for the color. For example, let's say you picked dark purple, code 660066. To change the font of all of the text to this color, write this:

```
<BODY TEXT=#660066>
This is the new colored font
</BODY>
```

See how easy it is? Just make sure you don't forget the hash mark, #. It's a symbol, so you don't need to worry about its meaning, just that it goes before the hexadecimal code.

You might want to go the simple route and just use text colors such as red, blue, and gray. Table 4.1 lists all of the colors and their respective hexadecimal codes.

Table 4.1 Text Colors and Hexadecimal Codes

Text Color	Color Code
Red	FF0000
Green	00FF00
Blue	0000FF
Yellow	FFFF00
Purple	800080
Fuchsia	FF00FF
Navy	000080
Teal	008080
Aqua	00FFFF
Olive	808000
Lime	00FF00
Black	000000
Silver	008000
Gray	808080
White	FFFFFF

Pretty cool, huh? You can use these colors without having to use the hexadecimal codes. These are interchangeable, meaning that setting COLOR equal to either #FFFFFF or "white" will make the text white.

In Figure 4.4, you can see a few of the most common colors in use. (This is WDFT04-02.html from the downloads.)

This document uses some common colors. Of course, this figure is in grayscale, but you can open up WDFT04-02.html on the companion Web site to see how the different colors look.

Now that you know how to change the color of your font and background, let's move on to some more <BODY> attributes.

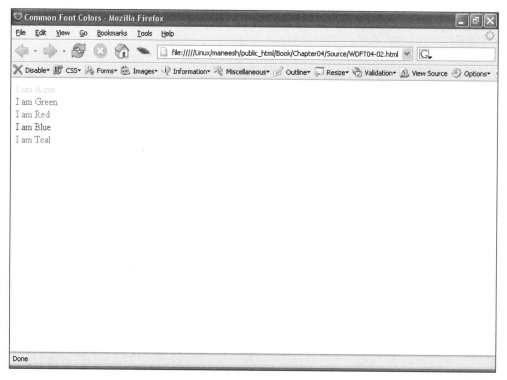

FIGURE 4.4 *Some common colors.*

Remember the BGCOLOR attribute? It allows you to change the background color of your page. In addition to BGCOLOR, <BODY> contains an attribute that lets you make an image the background.

What does this mean? Let's say you have an unobtrusive image you like, such as the one in Figure 4.5. (This image is bg04-01.gif on the companion Web site.) You want this image to be tiled across the background of your Web page, with all of your text and images on top of it.

FIGURE 4.5 *An unobtrusive background.*

Good news. The <BODY> tag has an attribute that does this! It's called BACKGROUND.

You use the BACKGROUND attribute like this:

```
<BODY BACKGROUND="location of image.jpg/gif">
```

This is a little bit different than defining the color of the background with BGCOLOR. Because you're using an image as the background, you need to provide a reference to the location of that image. You put this location between the quotation marks in the BACKGROUND attribute.

To find the location of the image, first you must save the HTML file. Then, find the location of the image relative to your HTML file on your computer.

For example, let's say you have a file called WDFT04-03.html, and you have an image called bg.gif that you want to use as the background. First, you create a folder called Images in the directory. The Images directory will be located under the HTML file, so that you have the HTML file located directly above the Images directory. Figure 4.6 shows the folder structure.

Place all of your images in this folder. Now you want to reference the background image, which is located in the Images subdirectory. To do this, simply refer to the image as Images\bg.gif. This tells the Web page and the browser that the background image will be located in the Images subdirectory and is called bg.gif.

This is called a *local reference*. We will discuss this later in the book. For now, just remember that to go from the HTML file's location to the folder with the image you want to use, just type the folder's name, a backslash, and the name of the image. This works no matter how many subdirectories you create.

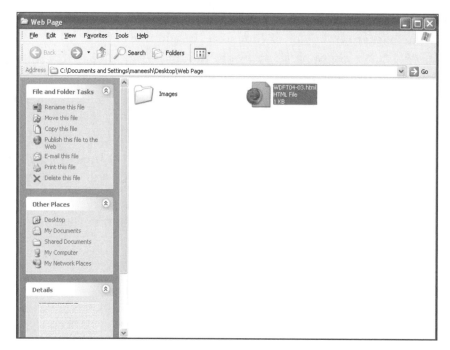

FIGURE 4.6 *Folder structure.*

To add this background to the page, use the BACKGROUND attribute. The following is the entire code listing for WDFT04-03.html:

```
<HTML>

<HEAD>
<TITLE>A Page That Has a Background Image</TITLE>
</HEAD>

<BODY BACKGROUND="Images\bg.gif">
I know not with what weapons World War III will be fought, but World War IV
will be fought with sticks and stones.
-Albert Einstein
</BODY>

</HTML>
```

As you can see, the most important part of this code is the <BODY> tag:

```
<BODY BACKGROUND="Images\bg.gif">
```

The BACKGROUND attribute determines the background image. Check out what it looks like in Figure 4.7.

The BACKGROUND attribute actually tiles the background image across the entire screen. Also, notice that the text appears on top of the background.

But what if the background image is really obtrusive and annoying? Figure 4.8 shows another background you could use.

Here's how to make this image your background (this is WDFT04-04.html on the companion Web site):

```
<BODY BACKGROUND="Images\bg2.jpg">
```

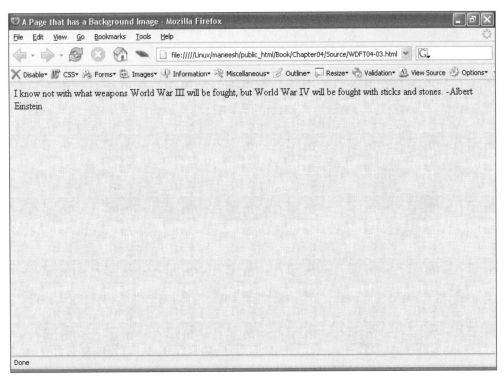

FIGURE 4.7 *Setting the background image.*

FIGURE 4.8 *A very obtrusive image.*

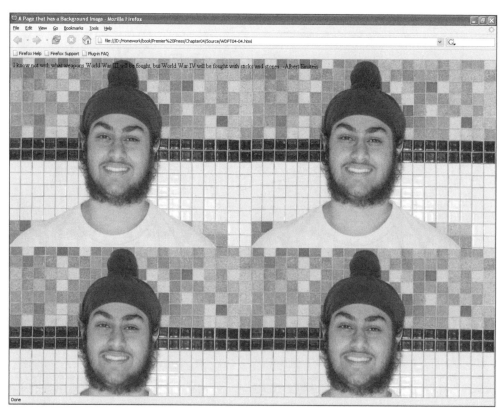

FIGURE 4.9 *An obtrusive background.*

You can barely see the text! The background is very obtrusive, rather annoying, and you're probably looking at it more than the text itself. This is due to the many colors, the numerous shapes, and the handsomeness of the subject. (Yeah, right.)

Maxim #5

"Never use an obtrusive background. Make sure that if you do use an image, it's pleasing to the eye."

Now that you know about background images, let's move on to the margin attributes. There are only two of them, but they have four names, so pay attention!

You've probably used Microsoft Word, right? As you're typing, notice that the writing doesn't begin at the very top of the page, but rather an inch or so down. The same thing happens on regular binder paper: There's a small margin at the top, bottom, left, and right. Figure 4.10 shows what these margins look like in Microsoft Word.

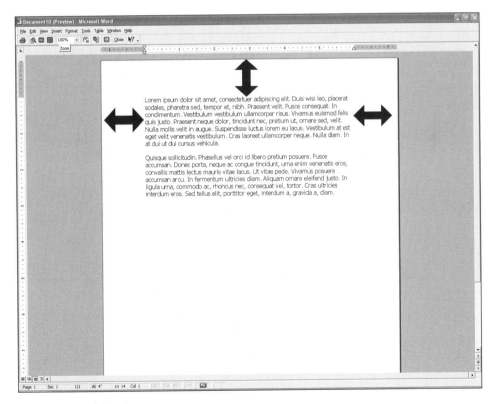

FIGURE 4.10 *Margins.*

These margins keep the page from being overloaded with information, and the page looks clean and easy to read.

The <BODY> tag allows you to define margins in Web pages as well. There are two margins that you can change, the top margin and the left margin. You cannot change the right or bottom margin, because they're automatically equal to the respective opposite margin. That is, the right margin is the same as the left, and the bottom margin is the same as the top.

Let's see how margins look when you use them on a Web page. Figure 4.11 shows an example. (This is WDFT04-05.html on the companion Web site.)

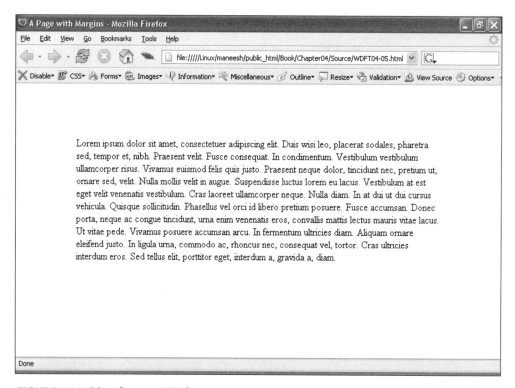

FIGURE 4.11 *Margins on a Web page.*

See how it works? The text is offset from the edges of the screen.

Actually *using* the attributes is a little tricky. Microsoft browsers recognize one attribute for margins, while other browsers recognize another attribute. To remedy this situation, you have to use the attributes for both Internet Explorer and the other browsers.

Internet Explorer uses `TOPMARGIN` and `LEFTMARGIN`:

`<BODY TOPMARGIN=x LEFTMARGIN=y>`

Of course, you need to change *x* and *y* to the size you want.

Other browsers use `MARGINHEIGHT` and `MARGINWIDTH`:

`<BODY MARGINHEIGHT=x MARGINWIDTH=y>`

Table 4.2 examines all of the margin settings.

TABLE 4.2 Margin Attributes

Attribute	Browser	Adjusts
`TOPMARGIN`	Internet Explorer	The top and bottom margins
`MARGINHEIGHT`	Everything else	The top and bottom margins
`LEFTMARGIN`	Internet Explorer	The left and right margins
`MARGINWIDTH`	Everything else	The left and right margins

Not too shabby, eh? Now all you need to know is what these measurements actually mean. In the case of margins, the browsers use pixels as the measurement. What's a pixel? It's the smallest standard of measure on a computer monitor. The size of a pixel varies with the resolution of the monitor, so usually it's easiest to test different widths and heights until you get what you want. Typically, the margins will be under 100 pixels, so start with that and fiddle around with it until you get good results.

The good news is that the margins in both Internet Explorer and the other browsers are measured in pixels, so you can use the same pixel count for each attribute.

Let's take a look at WDFT04-05.html, which uses margins:

```
<HTML>

<HEAD>
<TITLE>A Page with Margins</TITLE>
</HEAD>

<BODY TOPMARGIN=85 MARGINHEIGHT=85 LEFTMARGIN=100 MARGINWIDTH=100>
Text here
</BODY>

</HTML>
```

See the `<BODY>` tag? It uses all four of the attributes to create margins that are equal in Internet Explorer and in other browsers (Mozilla included). Compare Figure 4.11, which used margins in Mozilla Firefox, with Figure 4.12, which uses margins in Internet Explorer.

Almost exactly the same, right? Now if Microsoft would just accept every other browser's margin tags, we wouldn't need to worry about these double-named margins . . .

Those are all the `<BODY>` attributes we'll cover in this chapter. We'll talk about the rest of them when we get to hyperlinks in Chapter 6, "Hyperlinks, Lists, and Forms." Table 4.3 explains all of the attributes that we've covered so far.

TABLE 4.3 BODY Attributes

Attribute	Description
BGCOLOR	Sets the background color of the Web page
TEXT	Sets the default color of text on the Web page
BACKGROUND	Sets an image as the background of the page
TOPMARGIN/MARGINHEIGHT	Sets the top and bottom margins of the page
LEFTMARGIN/MARGINWIDTH	Sets the left and right margins of the page

Beautiful. With what you know now, you can easily create a simple page with text and color. Not too bad after reading only a few dozen pages!

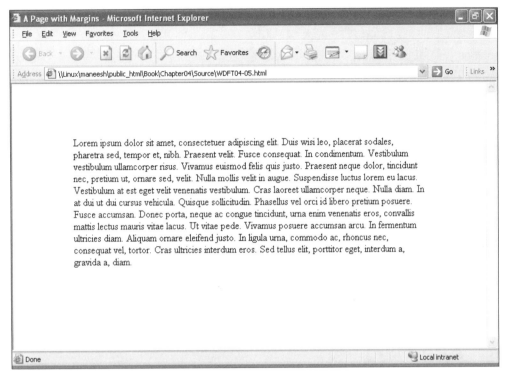

FIGURE 4.12 *Margins in Internet Explorer.*

Code Style

Let's talk about the style you use to write your code. You don't want it to be hard to read, do you?

Although we'll go over cleanliness later in this book, I want to give you a quick introduction before you start really writing code. These hints will allow others to understand the code you're writing. Not to mention that it will help you when you go back to the code later.

The most important thing to remember is to indent your HTML tags. When you have a tag that goes within another tag, press the Tab key before typing it in so it's indented. This makes it easier to close the tags at the end of the document.

For example, take the following code:

```
<HTML> <HEAD>
<TITLE>Bad Indentation</TITLE>
</HEAD>
<BODY>
<FONT COLOR=red>I am red <B>And I am Bold
</B>
</FONT>
<U>And I am Underlined
</U>
</BODY></HTML>
```

Not very pretty, eh? It's hard to tell which closing tags go with which opening tags. Now check out how it looks if you indent:

```
<HTML>

<HEAD>
    <TITLE>Good Indentation</TITLE>
</HEAD>

<BODY>

<FONT COLOR=red>I am red

    <B>And I am Bold
    </B>

</FONT>

    <U>And I am Underlined
    </U>

</BODY>

</HTML>
```

The indentation makes it easier to see what's going on. You know exactly which opening tag goes with which closing tag. It's also easier to understand what's going to appear on the screen.

Using indentation and proper spacing is important. If you do it right, you'll save a lot of time rereading code when you edit the file.

Another addition you can make: comments. These are explanatory asides that aren't read by the Web browser but can be seen in the source.

Comments

These are asides in an HTML document that aren't read by the browser but help others understand what's occurring in the code.

WHY USE COMMENTS?

Let's say you write some code and then come back to it six months later. It might not make any sense to you at all. Comments fix this problem. Include comments in your code to refresh your memory the next time you read it. Also, comments make your code easier to understand when someone else looks at it.

Now that you know *why* you should use comments, let's find out *how*.

All HTML comments begin with <!-- and end with -->. To add comments in HTML, you type what you want to say between <!-- and -->. For instance, take the WDFT04-01.html file from earlier in the chapter. I added comments and saved it as WDFT04-06.html on the companion Web site:

```
<HTML>

<!-- Begin Header -->
<HEAD>
<TITLE>Font Color Change in BODY Tag</TITLE>
</HEAD>
<!-- End Header -->

<!-- Begin Body, text is default gray -->
<BODY TEXT=gray>
```

```
This is the new colored font
</BODY>
<!-- End Body -->


</HTML>
```

See all the added comments? Figure 4.13 shows what the new page looks like.

It's exactly the same as Figure 4.2! That's the beauty of comments: They don't affect the actual page, but they really help in understanding what's going on in the code.

All right, let's move on to using Nvu.

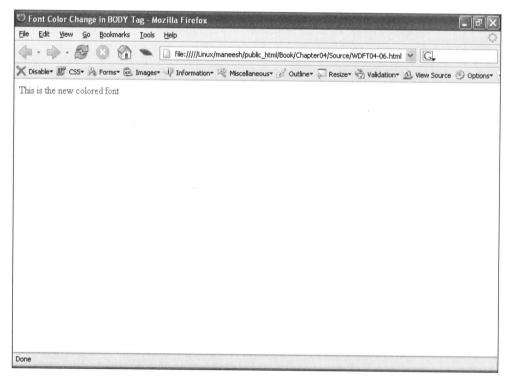

FIGURE 4.13 *Figure 4.2 with comments added.*

Nvu

In this section, I'm going to show you how to do everything you learned how to do in HTML much faster by using Nvu.

First of all, open up Nvu. It should look something like Figure 4.14.

You remember this page from Chapter 1, I'm sure.

First of all, select Format > Page Title and Properties. A window that looks like Figure 4.15 pops up.

Look at that! It takes care of the entire header for you. Type in something for the title. For this example, it's Chapter Four Web Page, as shown in Figure 4.16.

There are also a few other fields, such as Author, Description, and Language. These define the author and language of the page in the <HEAD></HEAD> sections, so that anyone who views the source knows who created the page and what it is about.

Click OK, and now the title has been set. A bit easier than typing it in HTML, huh?

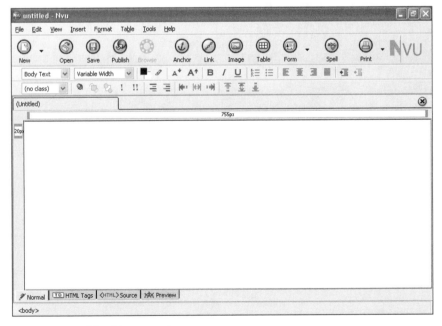

FIGURE 4.14 *The Nvu opening page.*

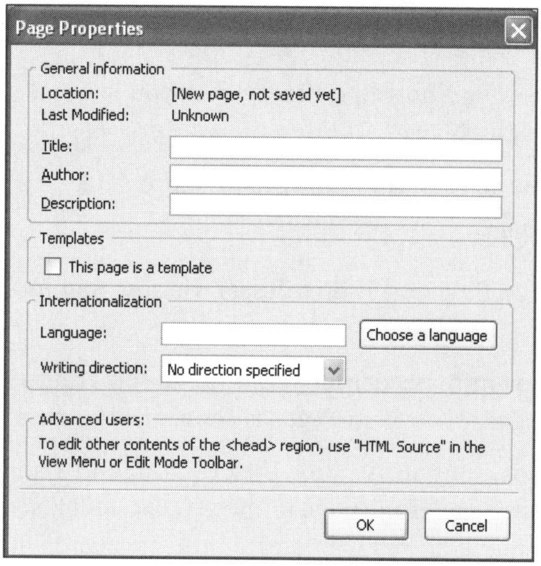

FIGURE 4.15 *The Page Properties window.*

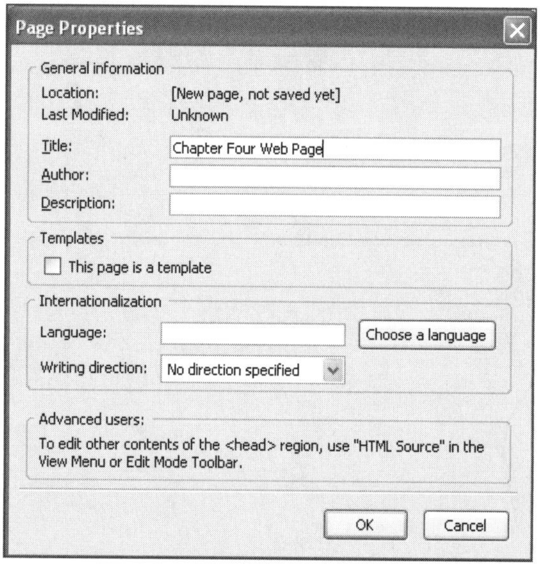

FIGURE 4.16 *The Page Properties window with the title filled in.*

Let's check out what you can do with actual BODY attributes. Select Format > Page Colors and Background. Figure 4.17 shows the window that pops up.

Awesome, huh? All you have to do is choose the colors you want. You can even set the background image by clicking Choose File at the bottom.

What if you want to change the margins? Click on Advanced Edit. Figure 4.18 shows the window that pops up.

Click on the Attribute drop-down list at the bottom, and check out everything you can select. Figure 4.19 shows you all the choices you have.

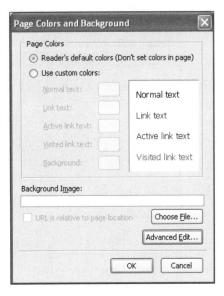

FIGURE 4.17 *The Page Colors and Background window.*

FIGURE 4.18 *The Advanced Property Editor window.*

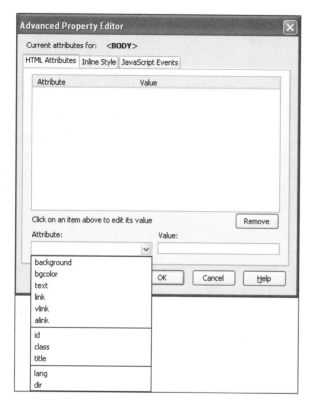

FIGURE 4.19 *The Attribute drop-down list.*

This includes every `<BODY>` attribute you could want. Choose `bgcolor` and set it to black. Then, set `text` to white. Click OK to exit.

Now enter the document section of the page and type "Hello, My name is [your name here]." Highlight your name and boldface it by clicking on the big B button on the toolbar. Another option is to highlight your name and press Ctrl+B.

You've just designed a Web page! Save it by choosing File > Save. Name it Chapter4.html. Open it up and see what you've made! Figure 4.20 shows the example created in this chapter. (This is Chapter4.html on the companion Web site.)

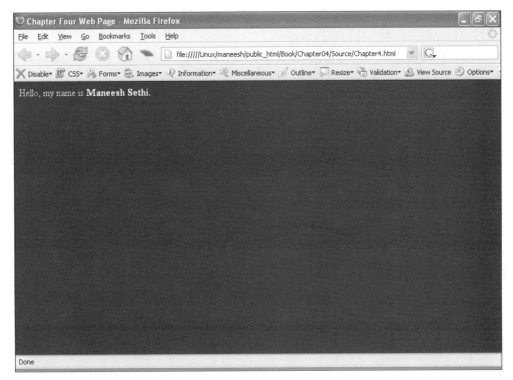

FIGURE 4.20 *The finished Web page, created in Nvu.*

That was pretty easy, huh? Now, let's check out how it looks in HTML. There are two ways to do this, and you already know both of them. You could open up the HTML file in Notepad, but the easier way is to click the HTML Source tab in Nvu. The program shows the source as follows:

```
<html>
<head>
<meta content="text/html; charset=ISO-8859-1"
http-equiv="content-type">
<title>Chapter Four Web Page</title>
</head>
```

```
<body style="color: white; background-color: black;" alink="#000099"
link="#000099" vlink="#990099">
Hello, my name is <span style="font-weight: bold;">Maneesh Sethi.</span><br>
</body>
</html>
```

Notice how much extra stuff there is in the file, such as the `<meta>` tag. The program automatically sets this, but oftentimes the information it adds is unnecessary and leads to cluttered HTML source. Also, the `<span>` tag is unnecessary, because there are much easier methods of bolding text.

But think about how much work Nvu just saved you. It might have taken you five minutes to type up this source by hand, but Nvu did it all for you!

Summary

That was a lot of fun! You learned a lot about HTML in this chapter:

❖ The basics of HTML

❖ Numerous BODY attributes

❖ How to use comments within code

❖ How to use Nvu

After all of this, you might be wondering why you even need to learn HTML at all. Why bother, when you can do it all in Nvu? Well, take a look at the code that Nvu made for you. It's bloated and rather ugly. That's because the program does everything it's told to do, but it doesn't make the code visually appealing. If you do the HTML yourself, though, the code will be much easier to understand. It also gives you greater control over what happens in your program.

Now get ready for the next chapter, where you'll learn how to insert images and format text.

Chapter 5

Working with Images and Text

Welcome to Chapter 5! In this chapter, you're going to learn a whole lot about images and text. You'll learn how to insert images into a Web page, how to size the images properly, and a little bit about editing images using JASC Paint Shop Pro. The text section will go over text alignment, formatting, and fonts.

This chapter is really important because it teaches you about graphics and text, the two most important things on a Web page. Heck, without them, a Web page would just be blank!

First things first. Let's learn about images.

What About Images?

You might already know a little about using images on a Web page. You use graphics to accentuate the page and make it look less boring. For example, Figure 5.1 shows one of the pages on my old Web site for my last book, *Game Programming for Teens*, at www.blitzprogramming.com.

See how the images and colors make the page more interesting to look at? If I got rid of the picture of the book at the top left and the graphical navigation bar at the top, the page would look pretty bare-bones and boring. The point of graphics is to make the Web experience more enjoyable.

FIGURE 5.1 *The www.BlizProgramming.com Web site.*

HTML uses several different image formats. (A format is a way of encoding an image so that Web browsers can view it.) You may have heard of bitmap (BMP) files, JPEG files, and GIF files. All

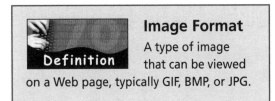

Image Format
A type of image
that can be viewed
on a Web page, typically GIF, BMP, or JPG.

three of these are viable image formats for use on a Web page. In addition, the PNG format is a newer image format that has been gaining ground in the past few years.

These three types of images should be used at different times. Table 5.1 examines the proper use of these formats.

TABLE 5.1 Image Formats

Format	When to Use	Size of File
BMP	When you need an image to be very high-quality	Very Large
JPG	When you want a full-color image that loads quickly	Medium
GIF	When you want an image with fewer colors that loads very quickly	Small

You'll hardly ever use bitmap images because of their large file sizes. They're only used when you need an image to be perfect, and on the Web it's best to sacrifice some quality for speed. These images have the suffix .bmp, so you might find an image called image.bmp.

Most online images are JPEGs. These images have the suffix .jpg or .jpeg, and typically they're full-color images that load quickly.

GIFs are used for clip art and other types of art that only use a few colors. They load extremely quickly and have a very small file size.

It's very important that you know the differences between these formats. Often, you can reduce a bitmap to a JPEG with little or no difference to the human eye. Let's take a look at the differences between a bitmap and a JPEG.

Figure 5.2 shows you the default Windows background in bitmap format.

FIGURE 5.2 *A bitmap image.*

As you can see, this full-color image is quite pretty. (It's blissbitmap.bmp on the companion Web site.) Yes, this image looks good, but guess how much storage space it takes? 1.37MB! This will take a good five minutes to load on an average 56k modem.

Let's compress the image into a JPEG to cut the file size. Compare Figure 5.2 with Figure 5.3, which is the same image in JPEG format.

Notice any difference? I'll bet you can't! This image is available on the companion Web site as blissjpeg.jpg. The compression on this image is hardly noticeable at all, yet the file size is only 66KB. That's only 4.8% the size of the bitmap!

Now, you might be wondering why the file size matters at all. Well, when someone visits your Web page, they can only download a certain amount of data at a time. The majority of Web users have narrowband 56k connections, which only allow downloads of about 5-6KB/second. So, it would take nearly five minutes to download the bitmap file, while it would take only a few seconds to download the JPEG image.

FIGURE 5.3 *The JPEG version of Figure 5.2.*

It's very likely that you'll be using compression quite often in Web design. You should probably learn a little about how to compress image files, then!

To compress an image, you need to use an imaging program like JASC Paint Shop Pro, which you can find at www.jasc.com/products. (They offer a free trial version.) Or, you can download a copy from my Web site (www.maneeshsethi.com). Just run the Paint Shop Pro executable file and go through the installation process. The window that pops up should look something like Figure 5.4.

Now you need to load the image to compress. Load blissbitmap.bmp from the Web site. The Paint Shop Pro window should look like Figure 5.5 now.

Since it's a full-color image, we're going to use JPEG compression. Go to File > Export > JPEG Optimizer. The JPEG Optimizer window is shown in Figure 5.6.

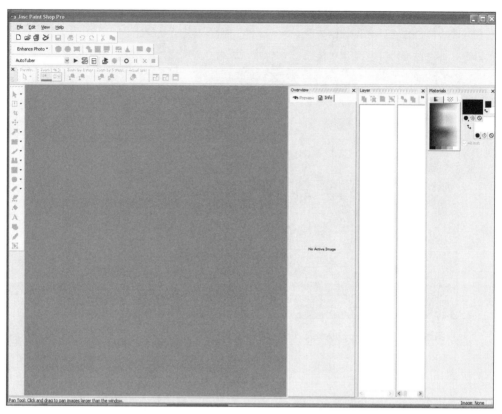

FIGURE 5.4 *The Paint Shop Pro interface.*

The image on the left is the uncompressed image, and the one on the right is the compressed JPEG image. In order to make the file size smaller, you need to adjust the compression value slider on the Quality tab.

Move the slider up until you notice a difference in the images. Then, move the slider down a few notches. This is the point where the image is compressed but hasn't lost a substantial amount of quality. In this case, the proper compression value is 15, but most images can be compressed even more and still look good.

Click on the Download Times tab and check out how quickly the image will load. Make sure it's very quick. You won't want it to take more than one or two seconds on a 56k modem. When the image looks the way you want it to look, click the OK button and choose where to save it.

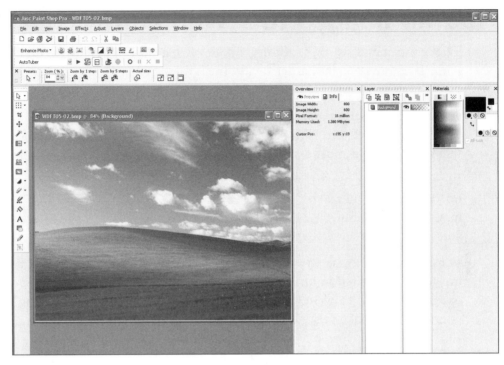

FIGURE 5.5 *An image file loaded in Paint Shop Pro.*

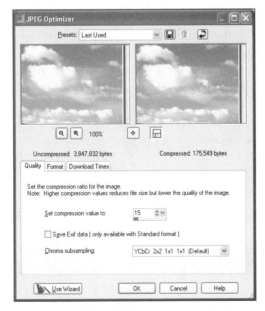

Now that you've created a compressed JPEG image, open it up. It should look identical to the uncompressed bitmap. If it still looks perfect, it's been compressed well.

Now that you know how to compress images, how about learning how to actually put them in an HTML document?

FIGURE 5.6 *The JPEG Optimizer window.*

Adding Images to a Web Page

The good news is that adding images to a Web page isn't that hard. Unfortunately, it's a bit harder to add them *correctly*.

First, you're going to learn how to place an image on a page using a new tag: `<IMG>`. This tag tells the Web browser that there's an image it must display.

> **Tag—`<IMG>`**
> This tells the browser that there's an image to be displayed. The `SRC` attribute is required.

In order to make the image appear onscreen, you need to include one mandatory attribute: `SRC`. This tells the browser where the image is located on your hard drive relative to the Web page.

For instance, let's say your Web page is located in a base directory, and image.jpg is located in an Images subdirectory. If you want to reference this image, you need to write the following in quotes: "Images/image.jpg". The entire line looks like this:

```
<IMG SRC="Images/image.jpg">
```

 note What are these crazy forward slashes? They're just a way of navigating through the folders to access the file that you need. You can organize your directories so that related files are in specific directories, and then you can access them with these forward slashes. If you need to move down through directories, type "*foldername/foldername/ . . . /filename*". There can be as many folders as you like. If you need to move up through the folder directories, use the .. symbol (two periods). In other words, if you're in Images and you need to reference something in the base folder, type "*../filename*". Again, you can use as many periods as you need to get to your destination. By the way, Web browsers use a different method of accessing files than your computer. You might have noticed that accessing files through your computer uses backslashes, but the Web uses forward slashes instead.

Pretty cool, huh? Check out what happens when you do this with the bitmap image from Figure 5.3. (This is WDFT05-01.html on the companion Web site.)

FIGURE 5.7 *Putting the blissjpeg.jpg image up on the Web.*

See that? The image appeared on the screen! Let's take a look at the source:

```
<HTML>

<HEAD>
<TITLE>Using an Image</TITLE>
</HEAD>

<BODY>
<!-- This is where the image is placed onscreen -->
<IMG SRC="Images/blissjpeg.jpg">
</BODY>

</HTML>
```

Not too shabby. The main section is the `<IMG>` tag, where the image is put on the screen.

Did you notice something strange about the `<IMG>` tag? That's right—it has no closing tag. The image doesn't actually modify anything onscreen, but rather performs an action on its own. Thus, it doesn't need a closing tag. There are a few other tags like `<IMG>`, and you'll learn about some of them later in this chapter.

There are a few important attributes of `<IMG>`, so let's look at them.

`<IMG>` Attributes

You already know about one required attribute: `SRC`. There's one more attribute that should appear in every image, although it's not strictly necessary. This is the `ALT` attribute.

`ALT` stands for alternate text, and it allows people who are blind or don't have an image-loading browser to read a description of the image. In addition, as you will learn more about in Part 4, search engines place value on `ALT` tags, and if you use them, your site may appear earlier on their search results.

How do you use `ALT`? Just add it to the `<IMG>` tag and make it equal to a phrase that describes the function of the image. The alternate text shouldn't describe what's *in* the image but rather the *job* of the image. For example, write something like "Navigate to Home" rather than "A blue box that says 'Home.'"

Let's try adding alternate text to the image you used earlier:

```
<IMG SRC="Images/blissjpeg.jpg" ALT="Welcome to the field">
```

Figure 5.8 shows what happens if you open up the image in Internet Explorer and hover your mouse over it. (This is WDFT05-02.html on the companion Web site.)

See that? The alternate text is displayed for anyone who wants information about the image.

There are a few more attributes, but they aren't really important enough to discuss. Table 5.2 lists all of them.

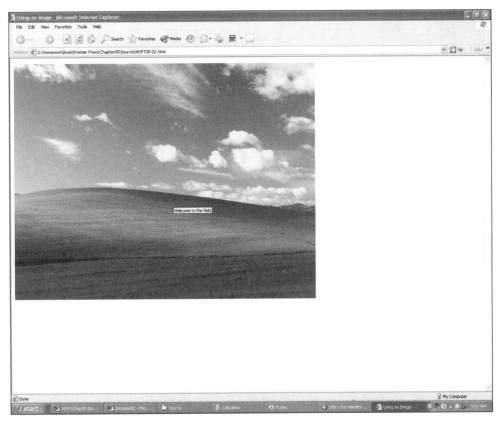

FIGURE 5.8 *Using alternate text.*

TABLE 5.2 `<IMG>` **Attributes**

Attribute	Description
WIDTH	The width of the image in pixels. Specifying the width helps the page load faster.
HEIGHT	The height of the image in pixels. Specifying the height helps the page load faster.
ALIGN (top|middle| bottom|left|right)	Allows you to choose where the image is located onscreen.
BORDER	The thickness of the border.

There are a few more, such as image maps, but I won't be going over them in this book.

If you know the pixel width and height of your image (you can find them by right-clicking on them in a browser and in Paint Shop Pro), adding that information to your image will make the page load a little faster. It's always good to add the WIDTH and HEIGHT if possible.

ALIGN allows you to move the image around the page. Tables are a better way to work with images, however, and I don't recommend using ALIGN.

The last attribute, BORDER, allows you to create a border around the image. Compare Figure 5.7 with Figure 5.9, which has a border. (This is WDFT05-03.html on the companion Web site.)

FIGURE 5.9 *Using a border around an image.*

It looks pretty cool, huh? It's a nice effect when you want to make an image look a little stylish.

That's about it for the `<IMG>` tag. Now you know how to insert images into a Web page. Let's quickly go over how to find images to use.

Procuring Images

When you're designing a Web page, think about what types of images you want to use. After you've decided, make them yourself! Try drawing them or designing them in Paint Shop Pro. If you can't, and you don't know anyone who can, you can find clip art or royalty-free images on the Web.

A good place to look is Google Image Search. Go to images.google.com and search for whatever you want. If you find an image you like, however, you *cannot* use it without asking for permission. Go to the owner's Web site and ask if it's okay to use the image.

Also, another good resource is http://dgl.microsoft.com. This is Microsoft's clip art page, and if you use Microsoft Word, you already have access to many of the clip art files. Just open Microsoft Word and select Insert > Picture > Clip Art. Figure 5.10 shows the window that pops up.

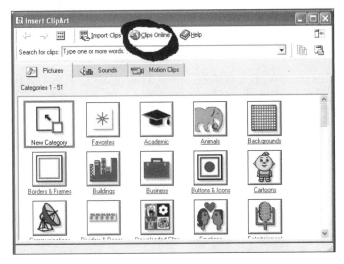

FIGURE 5.10 *The ClipArt window in Microsoft Word.*

Click on the Clips Online button to open the Microsoft Online ClipArt Gallery, which has a lot of really cool pictures and images.

Unfortunately, if you really want professional images, you're going to have to pay extra for them. Two of the best sites for images are photos.com and corbis.com. You can find some cool images, but it'll lighten your wallet.

That's about it for procuring images. Next up, we're going to learn about text!

Text Time

Text is a very important part of Web design. Obviously, everything you read is made up of text. In order to make it readable, you need to emphasize some parts, make other parts bigger, and so on.

This section looks at three aspects of text: formatting, alignment, and fonts. Let's start off with text formatting.

Text Formatting

What does text formatting entail? Basically, it means emphasizing some words more than others. The most common ways to emphasize text are boldface, italics, and underlining.

Boldface text is very common on the Web. All this means is making some words darker than others to emphasize them. For example, **this text is boldface**. When you use boldface words on a Web page, the viewer's eyes are automatically drawn to them.

Figure 5.11 shows a Web page with boldface text. (This is WDFT05-04.html on the companion Web site.)

Your eyes were automatically drawn to the words "nice website that you like" because they're boldface. This really emphasizes that part of the text.

Before I show you how to use boldface, there's a new maxim to introduce:

When you use too much boldface, your reader doesn't even notice it anymore. Save it for the most important sections of your code.

Maxim #6
"Don't overuse boldface. It won't help."

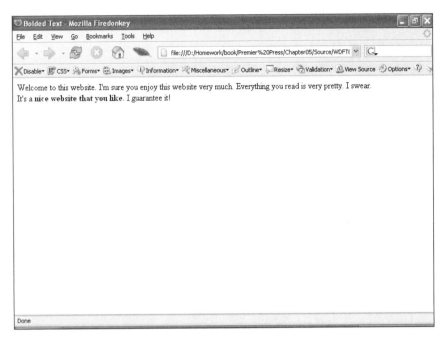

FIGURE 5.11 *Boldface text.*

There are two tags you can use, <B> and <STRONG>. Both of these tags do the same thing.

Let's look at the code for WDFT05-04.html, which was shown in Figure 5.11. It uses the <B> tag:

> **Tags—<B> </B> and <STRONG> </STRONG>**
> These make the affected text boldface.

```
<HTML>

<HEAD>
<TITLE>Boldface Text</TITLE>
</HEAD>

<BODY>
Welcome to this Web site. I'm sure you'll enjoy this Web site very much.
Everything you read here is very pretty. I swear.
<BR> It's a <B>nice Web site that you'll like.</B> I guarantee it!
</BODY>

</HTML>
```

The most important line is the third one from the bottom:

```
<BR> It's a <B>nice Web site that you'll like.</B> I guarantee it!
```

By bracketing a section of text with the `<B>` and `</B>` tags, you make it boldface. (Don't worry about the `<BR>` tag; we'll discuss that later on in the chapter.)

Now, boldface isn't the only way to emphasize text. Let's go over italics.

Italics slant the text a little so it stands out. *This text is in italics.* Let's modify the previous example using italics.

You can create italics with either `<I>/</I>` or `<EM>/</EM>`. I usually use the `<I>` tags, but you can choose for yourself.

To italicize text, bracket it with the `<I>` and `</I>` tags:

> **Tags—`<I> </I>` and `<EM> </EM>`**
>
> These make the text italicized, so it's tilted slightly.

```
<I> This is italicized</I> but this is not.
```

The text inside the `<I>` tags is italicized. Figure 5.12 shows what this text looks like on a Web browser. (This is WDFT05-05.html on the companion Web site.)

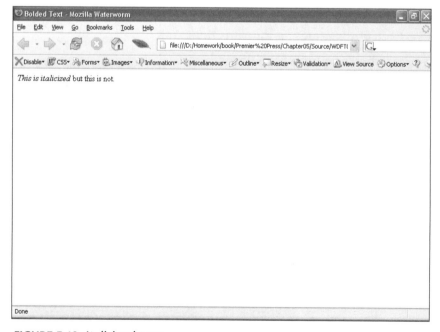

FIGURE 5.12 *Italicized text.*

Pretty easy. Now, what if you want to italicize text *and* boldface it?

To do this, you need to use the "stack and pop" method of writing tags. When you modify a section of text using a tag, you need to close the tag directly after that section. But when you add another tag inside *that* tag, you need to close that tag *before* closing the other one.

For example, here's how to boldface and italicize text:

```
<B><I>Boldfaced and Italicized</I></B>
```

This is the wrong way to do it:

```
<B><I>Boldfaced and Italicized</B></I>
```

The first tag you open needs to be the last tag you close. Keep in mind, you can reverse the tags so that `<I>` appears before `<B>`, but then you need to close the `<I>` tag first.

Figure 5.13 shows what boldfaced and italicized text looks like. (This is WDFT05-06.html on the companion Web site.)

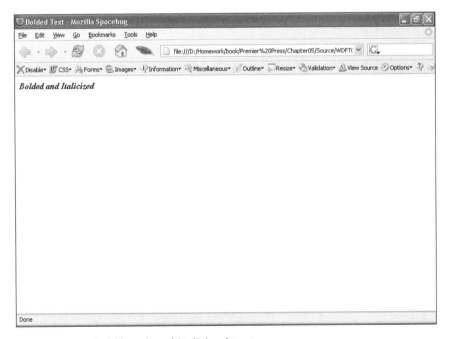

FIGURE 5.13 *Boldfaced and italicized text.*

There are a few more methods of emphasizing text. The first one is underlining, using the `<U>` and `</U>` tags. You can also use strikethrough, where a horizontal line is drawn through the text. That uses the `<S>` and `</S>` tags.

> **Tag—`<U>` `</U>`**
> This underlines the affected text.

> **Tag—`<S>` `</S>`**
> This draws a strikethrough line through the affected text.

The last way of emphasizing text is through headers. Remember Chapter 3, which discussed headers? There are six different sizes of headers, each smaller than the previous one. Figure 5.14 shows all of the headers. (This is WDFT05-07.html on the companion Web site.)

Yeah, you've seen this image before, but it demonstrates the differences between the headers. To use a header, you use these tags: `<H1>`, `<H2>`, `<H3>`, `<H4>`, `<H5>`, or

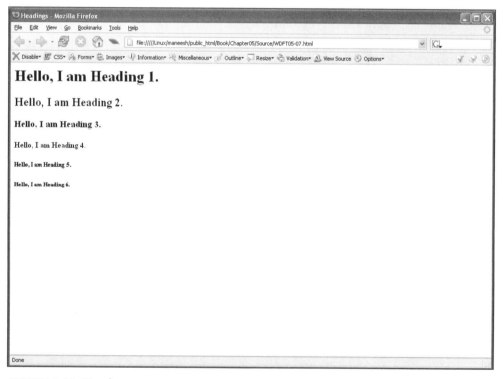

FIGURE 5.14 *Headers.*

<H6>. The higher the number, the smaller the header, so <H1> is the biggest and <H6> is the smallest. Headers are good for emphasizing certain sections of text, like I've been doing in this book!

That's it for text formatting. Let's move on to text alignment.

Text Alignment

The first thing you need to learn about align-ment is how to create paragraphs using the <P> tag. The cool thing about this tag is that it takes care of the spacing for you!

> **Tag—<P> </P>**
> This begins a new paragraph.

Take a look at Figure 5.15, which shows a page with two paragraphs. (This is WDFT05-08.html on the companion Web site.)

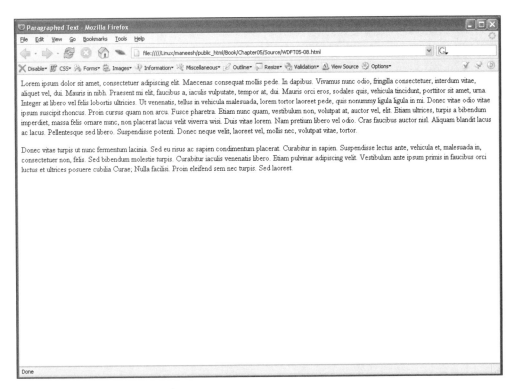

FIGURE 5.15 *Two paragraphs.*

You don't have to close the `<P>` tag. That is, `</P>` is unnecessary. It's allowed but not required.

Now, let's align this text! `<P>` has an `ALIGN` attribute that lets you align the text to the right, center, or left.

Originally, the code was

```
<P> Lorem ipsum...
<P> Donec vitae...
```

Let's change this so the first paragraph aligns to the right and the second aligns to the center, as in Figure 5.16. (This is WDFT05-09.html on the companion Web site.)

```
<P ALIGN=right> Lorem ipsum...
<P ALIGN=center> Donec vitae...
```

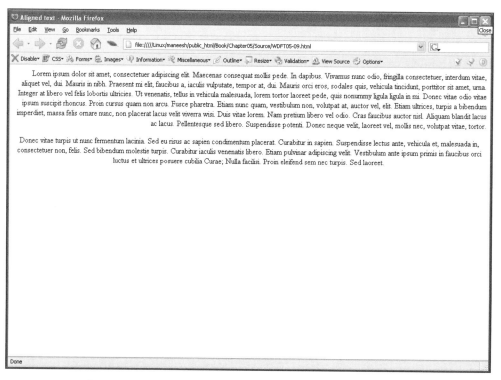

FIGURE 5.16 *Aligning right and center.*

See the difference? The first paragraph has the text lined up on the right, and the second paragraph is centered.

What if you want to align more than just one paragraph to the center or to the right? Use the ⟨DIV⟩ tag, with ALIGN equaling right or center. As with ⟨P⟩, left-alignment is the default.

> **Tag—⟨DIV⟩ ⟨/DIV⟩**
> This tag allows you to align more than one paragraph at a time.

So, if you wanted both paragraphs in Figure 5.16 to be right-aligned, you'd write this:

```
<DIV ALIGN=right> Lorem ipsum...
<P> Donec vitae...
</DIV>
```

Another way to create paragraphs is to use the ⟨BR⟩ tag, which puts in an automatic line break. This is extremely useful, and I use it a lot in my HTML design. This tag doesn't require a closing tag.

> **Tag—⟨BR⟩**
> This adds a line break to the page.

One more thing before we finish up this section. Remember margins? Sometimes you want a section of text to have deeper margins, but you don't want to add the margins to the ⟨BODY⟩ tag. A way to get around this is to use the ⟨BLOCKQUOTE⟩ tag.

> **Tag—⟨BLOCKQUOTE⟩ ⟨/BLOCKQUOTE⟩**
> This gives a section of text deeper margins.

Figure 5.17 shows how these two paragraphs look using ⟨BLOCKQUOTE⟩ (This is WDFT05-10.html on the companion Web site.)

It looks pretty nice, huh? It keeps your eyes from moving off the page as you read.

That's about it for text alignment. Next up, we're going to learn all about fonts.

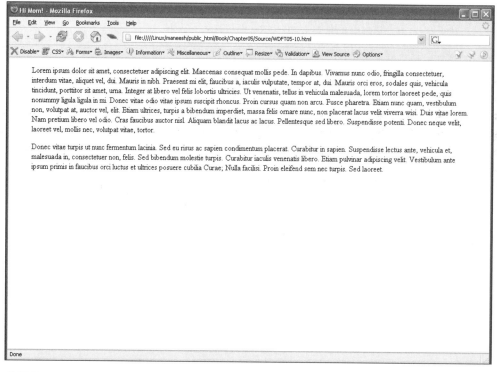

FIGURE 5.17 `<BLOCKQUOTE>`.

Fonts

Fonts are kind of an important aspect of text. Using different font sizes allows you to emphasize one part of your page over another, and different fonts can be used for different sections of your page.

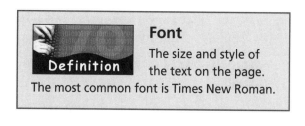

Font
The size and style of the text on the page. The most common font is Times New Roman.

Let's first go over font size. The size of a font determines how big text appears onscreen. The actual, absolute size will vary depending on the size of the monitor and the screen resolution, but a larger font size will always be larger than a smaller font.

Typical font sizes range from 1 to 8, but you can go a little smaller or bigger if necessary. How do you adjust font size? You use the <FONT> tag, of course!

> **Tag—<FONT> </FONT>**
> This allows you to adjust the font's size, face, and color.

No matter what font size you use, keep everything proportional. You don't want 10-point type right before 3-point type, as shown in Figure 5.18. (This is WDFT05-11.html on the Web site.)

As you can see, these two font sizes are very different. In most cases, you don't want text that's next to each other to deviate by more than one or two font sizes. Most commonly, you'll use a font size of 3 on your companion Web pages.

To adjust the font, use the <FONT> tag with the SIZE attribute. For example, here's how to set a certain line of text to a font size of 6:

```
<FONT SIZE=6>I am a line of text that is font size 6!</FONT>
```

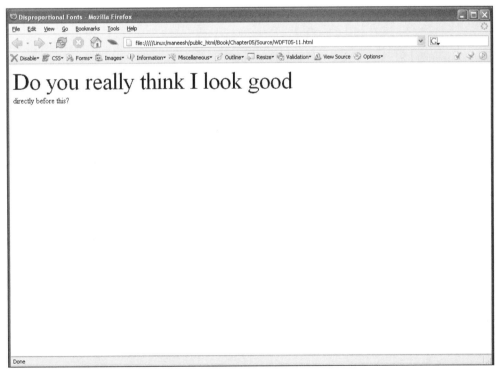

FIGURE 5.18 *Disproportional font sizes.*

What if you want to adjust the font color? You already did this a while ago, but let me refresh your memory.

To adjust the color, use the `COLOR` attribute. You can set this equal to a hexadecimal value, as you learned in the previous chapter, or you can use one of the 16 predefined colors. Let's say you want some text that's blue and a font size of 5. Your code will look something like this:

```
<FONT COLOR=blue SIZE=5> I am font 5 and blue text!</FONT>
```

This will look like Figure 5.19. (This is WDFT05-12.html on the companion Web site.) By the way, you won't be able to see color in the book, but you can see the real file on the companion Web site.

Pretty easy, eh?

The last thing that you can adjust using `<FONT>` is the font face, which is another name for the font type. This is usually Times New Roman, but you can adjust it using the `<FONT>` tag.

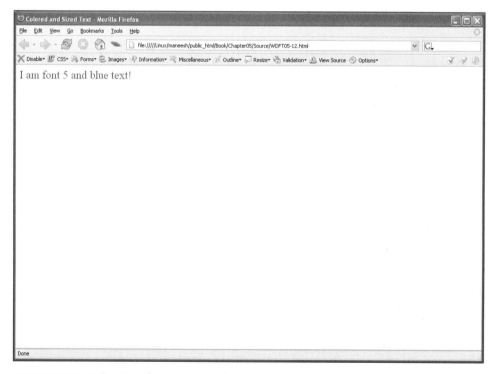

FIGURE 5.19 *Adjusting font color and size.*

Here's how to adjust the font face:

```
<FONT FACE=arial> I am Arial
text!</FONT>
```

It's pretty easy. Look at difference between Arial and Times New Roman in Figure 5.20. (This is WDFT05-13.html on the companion Web site.)

Let's take a look at the code:

```
<HTML>

<HEAD>
<TITLE>Boldfaced Text</TITLE>
</HEAD>

<BODY>
<FONT FACE=arial SIZE=5> I Am Arial!</FONT>
<BR>
<FONT FACE="times new roman" SIZE=5> I am Times New Roman!</FONT>

</BODY>

</HTML>
```

FIGURE 5.20 *Arial and Times New Roman.*

Obviously, the most important part is the `<FONT>` sections. Notice how I put `"times new roman"` in quotes, because it's more than two words.

The following are the most common fonts you'll use:

A font will show up on the visitor's screen only if it's installed on their computer. Because of this, stick to the very common fonts that are available on all computers.

❖ Times New Roman
❖ Garamond
❖ Arial
❖ Helvetica
❖ Georgia

I recommend sticking to Times New Roman almost always.

Table 5.3 examines all of the `<FONT>` attributes.

TABLE 5.3 Font Attributes

Attribute	Description
SIZE	Adjusts the size of the font.
COLOR	Changes the color of the text.
FACE	Adjusts the font or typeface of the text.

Before we finish the chapter, I want to talk about one last thing: special characters.

Special Characters

Sometimes you may want to use a special character, like a copyright symbol or a fraction sign. Fortunately, HTML allows you to use some special characters.

There's a complete reference in Appendix A, but let's go over a few of these special characters:

- ❖ For a cent sign, type &cent.
- ❖ For a greater-than sign, type &gt. For a less-than sign, type &lt.
- ❖ For a plus/minus sign, type &plusmn.
- ❖ For an accented e, type &eacute.

Summary

Whoo! That was a tough chapter. Don't worry about it, though, cause we are learning a lot about HTML.

In this chapter you learned the following:

- ❖ The differences between image formats
- ❖ How to compress an image in Paint Shop Pro
- ❖ How to add an image to a Web page
- ❖ All about <IMG> attributes
- ❖ How to find images
- ❖ How to align and format text
- ❖ How to adjust the text's font size, color, and face
- ❖ How to use special characters

That was a lot of stuff. Now get ready the for next chapter, on links, lists, and forms.

Chapter 6

Hyperlinks, Lists, and Forms

Welcome to Chapter 6. This chapter is going to teach you about hyperlinks, lists, and forms. These items, especially hyperlinks, are everywhere on the Internet, so it's very important to learn all about how they work and what they do.

This chapter is going to teach you almost everything you need to know about HTML (besides a little bit about tables and some other stuff in the next chapter). We've got a lot of stuff to do, so we better get moving!

Hyperlinks

Hyperlinks are the backbone of the Internet. Otherwise known as simply *links*, these items make the Web work.

What's a hyperlink? It's a way of navigating from one place to another. It's like a map. When you click on a hyperlink, you're following that map from point A to point B.

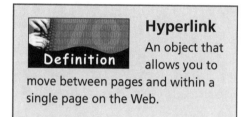

Hyperlink
An object that allows you to move between pages and within a single page on the Web.

Hyperlinks allow you to have more than one page on your Web site, and visitors can move between the pages using them. I know you've seen hyperlinks on the Internet because they're used on almost every single Web page.

Let's go back to www.maneeshsethi.com and take a look at the hyperlinks.

FIGURE 6.1 *Hyperlinks within www.maneeshsethi.com.*

See those words with underlined text? Those are hyperlinks. Try visiting the Web page and clicking on some of the underlined words to follow the hyperlinks.

Now let's find out how to make a link. Another name for a hyperlink is an *anchor*, and the HTML tag for it is `<A></A>`.

> **Tag—`<A></A>`**
> This tells the browser that an anchor is being used; that is, either a link or a named anchor.

This tag requires at least one attribute. For normal hyperlinks, this is HREF, which stands for "hypertext reference." This is just another name for a link that allows you to go from one page to another. The HREF attribute is always set equal to the location of the file to which you want to link.

Take a look at the following code, which shows how a link works:

```
<HTML>

<HEAD>
<TITLE>Using Links</TITLE>
</HEAD>

<BODY>
The following is a set of links.
<P>

Go to <A HREF="http://www.cnn.com">CNN</A> for news!
<BR>
Visit <A HREF="http://www.maneeshsethi.com">ManeeshSethi.com </A> for questions about this book!


</BODY>
</HTML>
```

This page ends up looking like Figure 6.2. (This is WDFT06-01.html on the companion Web site.)

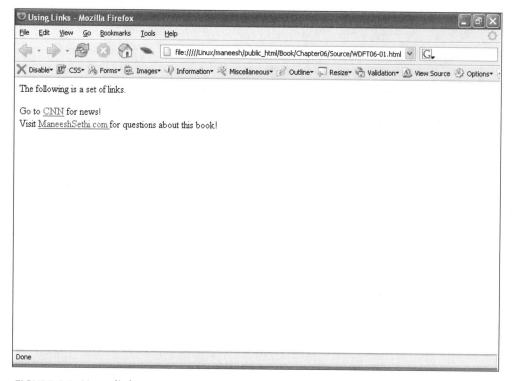

FIGURE 6.2 *Hyperlinks.*

Let's talk about the formation of the link. The CNN link looks like this:

```
Go to <A HREF="http://www.cnn.com">CNN</A> for news!
```

Notice that the <A HREF="..."> is in the middle of a sentence. That's okay if you only want the link to be a few words. The HREF attribute is set equal to the Web site, and then some of the text goes within the <A> and </A> tags. This modified text is what you click to navigate to the page. It's the link.

Notice that this link is very different from all other references and links that you've used in the past. This is called an *absolute link*, while the <IMG> reference that we went over in the last chapter was called a *relative link*.

Linking text in Nvu involves the link button on the main task bar. Just click the button and a window pops up asking you for the link text. Type in link text and the location to be linked to, and a link is created.

WHAT'S THE DIFFERENCE BETWEEN
RELATIVE AND ABSOLUTE LINKS?

Relative and absolute links are used for different purposes. Typically, you'll use a relative link to get from one page on your Web site to another on the same site. For example, if you had a Web page named index.html and you wanted a link to aboutme.html, you would use a relative link: `<A HREF="aboutme.html">`.

If you're linking to an external site, such as CNN.com, you format it in a different way. With absolute links, you need to add "`http://`" (which stands for Hypertext Transfer Protocol) to the link. This tells the Web browser that the link is external and will take the user outside this Web site. That's why the link in the preceding document says `HREF="http://www.cnn.com"` rather than just `cnn.com`.

So now you can link text. But guess what? There are different types of text links: normal, visited, and active. Each one is a different color. A normal link is simply a regular text link, a visited link is one that the user has clicked on, and an active link is one that the user is in the process of clicking.

Remember when I promised you that there would be a few more `<BODY>` attributes? Well, here they are. By adding some new attributes, you can adjust the colors of all three types of links.

By default, the normal link color is blue, the visited link color is purple, and the active link color is dark blue. But what if you have a black background on a page? These colors don't stand out very well. In that case, you can add three attributes to `<BODY>` to get better colors: `LINK`, `ALINK`, and `VLINK`.

For instance, let's say you want to change the default colors of the links: white for normal, yellow for active, and red for visited. Your `<BODY>` tag will probably look like this:

```
<BODY LINK=white VLINK=red ALINK=yellow>
```

Pretty simple, eh? Check out WDFT06-02.html on the companion Web site, which has these colors on a black background. It looks a little like Figure 6.3.

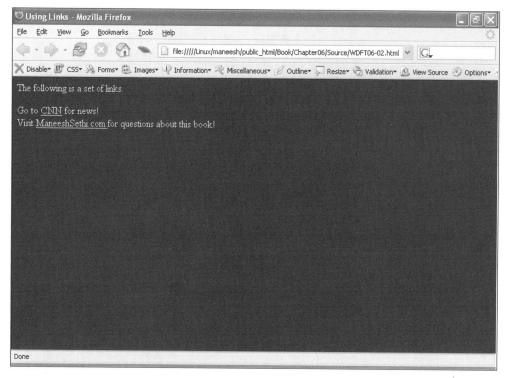

FIGURE 6.3 *Colored hyperlinks.*

Table 6.1 defines these new attributes.

TABLE 6.1 The Remaining Body Attributes

Tag	Description
LINK	The color of a basic link.
VLINK	The color of a visited link.
ALINK	The color of an active link.

Now, when should you use colored links? Try to use them as sparingly as possible, because everyone who uses the Internet is used to blue links. When you change the color, people get confused. They might even think that the linked text isn't a link.

Remember, never ever make your page more confusing than it has to be. Don't forget Maxim #2 from Chapter 2: "Never make the visitor work harder than he has to. Even better, never make the visitor work. Period."

Alright, so that's it for links, for now. You'll learn a little bit more about links in Chapter 9, "Navigation," because navigation uses more links than anything else.

Lists

Let's talk a little bit about lists. Lists are pretty simple, and they don't take up much time. In addition, they're very easy to use.

Lists are just sets of data that are related. If you've ever taken bullet point notes in class or read a recipe, you've used a list.

HTML has three types of lists: ordered, unordered, and definition. Let's go over all of them.

Bullet Lists

You've probably seen bullet point lists. They look like this:

❖ Item 1
❖ Item 2
❖ Item 3

This is extremely useful when you need to present a set of data to the reader. You can use it to outline specific points and summarize information.

In HTML, a bullet list is called an *unordered* list. You use the <UL></UL> tag to define an unordered list. Within the <UL></UL> tag, you use the <LI></LI> tag to define elements in the list. Let's look at WDFT06-03.html on the companion Web site:

```
<HTML>

<HEAD>
<TITLE>Bullet Lists</TITLE>
</HEAD>

<BODY>
<UL>
```

> **Tag—<UL></UL>**
> This sets up an unordered (bullet point) list.

```
        <LI>I am the first element!</LI>
        <LI>I am the second element!</LI>
        <LI>Look at me, I am number 3!</LI>
</UL>


</BODY>
</HTML>
```

This is shown in Figure 6.4.

As you can see, setting up a list requires both the list type tag (`<UL></UL>`) and the individual item tag (`<LI></LI>`). There's an individual item tag for both unordered and ordered lists.

That's it for bullet point lists. Let's move on to numbered lists.

Numbered Lists

Numbered lists, otherwise known as *ordered* lists, are almost exactly the same as bullet point lists. The only differences are that the tag is different (`<OL></OL>` rather than `<UL></UL>`) and it uses numbers rather than bullet points. You'll probably use numbered lists when you want to give instructions or teach the user how to do something.

Pretty simple, eh? Let's see how it works.

```
<OL>
        <LI>I am the first action in a
series.</LI>
        <LI>I am the second.</LI>
        <LI>Check it out, I do the last
thing!</LI>
</OL>
```

Figure 6.5 shows how it looks. (This is WDFT06-04.html on the companion Web site.)

Tag—`<LI></LI>`
This defines the items within a list.

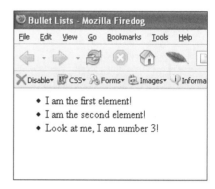

FIGURE 6.4 *An unordered list.*

Tag—`<OL></OL>`
This sets up an ordered (numbered) list.

FIGURE 6.5 *An ordered list.*

Notice how the HTML takes care of the numbering automatically: the first item is number 1, the second is number 2, and so on.

Okay, let's look at the last type of lists: definition lists.

Definition Lists

Definition lists are a little different than ordered and unordered lists. Typically, they're not used to summarize or show information in a concise manner, but rather to explain an idea or define an item. Also, unlike the previous types of lists, definition lists don't use the `<LI></LI>` tag.

To set up a definition list, you use the `<DL></DL>` tag. This tag borders the entire list. For each item, you need to use the `<DT></DT>` tag for the item that's defined and the `<DD></DD>` tag for the definition.

> **Tag—`<DL></DL>`**
> This sets up a definition list.

Huh? That's right, there are three parts to the definition list, and you need to use all of them to create a proper definition.

Figure 6.6 shows what a definition list looks like. (This is WDFT06-05.html on the companion Web site.)

See? Each item has two parts, the header and the definition. `<DT>` means "definition title," while `<DD>` means "definition definition." You gotta love redundancy, eh?

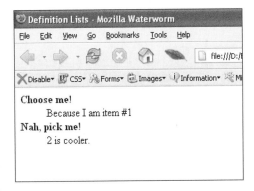

FIGURE 6.6 *A definition list.*

> **Tag—`<DT></DT>`**
> This creates an item that will be defined within a definition list.

> **Tag—`<DD></DD>`**
> This defines an item within a definition list.

Let's see the code that made Figure 6.6:

```
<BODY>
<DL>
     <DT><B>Choose me!</B></DT>
     <DD> Because I am item #1 </DD>
     <DT><B>Nah, pick me!</B></DT>
     <DD>2 is cooler.</DD>

</DL>
</BODY>
```

Notice that the `<DT></DT>` items are bolded so that they stand out.

WHEN SHOULD I USE A DEFINITION LIST?

Definition lists are definitely (pun intended) used less often than ordered and unordered lists. However, there are still times when you should use them.

They're great when you're defining words or items, of course. If you ever need to explain something to your reader, a definition list works very well. Also, you can use definition lists when selling a product. For example, you might have a list where the definition title is "High Quality" and the definition definition says, "Our 40-year history allows us to offer you better service." Using definition tags helps emphasize your points.

Nesting

Before we move on from lists, I want to talk about *nesting*. This allows you to put lists within lists so that you can have items and sub-items. It might be easier to explain with an example.

Let's say you're putting a recipe on your site. You want to create a section for ingredients and a section for preparation steps. You can use lists to make the recipe look a lot better.

The following code shows how you'd publish a recipe:

```
<DL>
     <DT><B>Ingredients:</B><DT>
     <DD><UL>
```

```
<LI>1 cup sugar</LI>
<LI>1 teaspoon water</LI>
<LI>1 pound spaghetti</LI>
<LI>3 scoops ice cream</LI>

 </UL></DD>

<DT><B>Procedure:</B></DD>
<DD><OL>

<LI>Put spaghetti in pan</LI>
<LI>Add sugar and water</LI>
<LI>Stir for fifteen minutes</LI>
<LI>Add ice cream</LI>
<LI>Simmer and eat</LI>

</OL></DD>
```

```
</DL>
```

See how the items are nested? This places some items under other items to make the list easier to read. Figure 6.7 shows you what the recipe looks like. (This is WDFT06-06.html on the companion Web site.)

Please don't use this recipe. I've tried it before, and believe me: Just because spaghetti and ice cream taste good doesn't mean they taste good *together*.

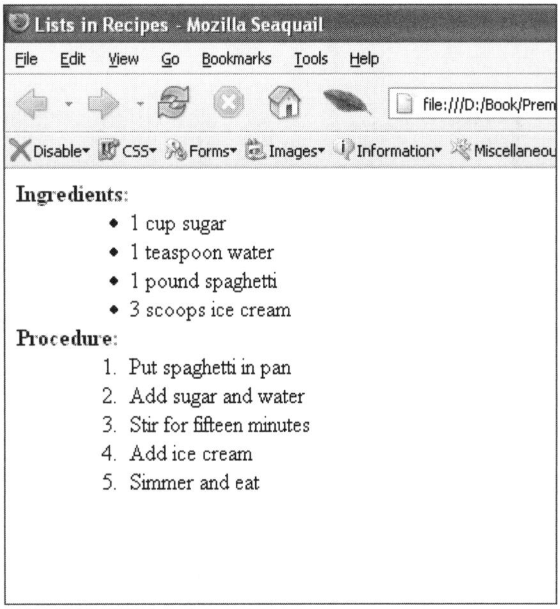

FIGURE 6.7 *A nested list.*

Want to make a list using Nvu? Let's try it. Open up Nvu and type whatever you want to put in your list. After that, just highlight the text, open up the Format menu, and navigate to the List category. Choose the type of list you want from the menu. Figure 6.8 shows the menu.

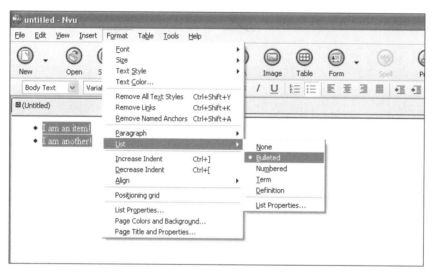

FIGURE 6.8 *Setting up a list in Nvu.*

Whoo! That's all you need to know about lists. Let's move on to something a little more difficult: forms.

Forms

Sweet, we're on the last section of the chapter! Forms are actually among the most complex items on Web sites. You can't achieve the full power of the Web using only HTML. You have to use a different type of language to actually submit the forms.

Some common languages are PHP and Perl. Unfortunately, these are both difficult to learn and require their own book. But luckily, there are lots of free CGI and PHP documents online!

We'll talk about these languages a little more later in this chapter. Right now, let's talk about forms. The best way to describe a form is to show you. Figure 6.9 shows a form from one of my older sites, sikhtemple.org.

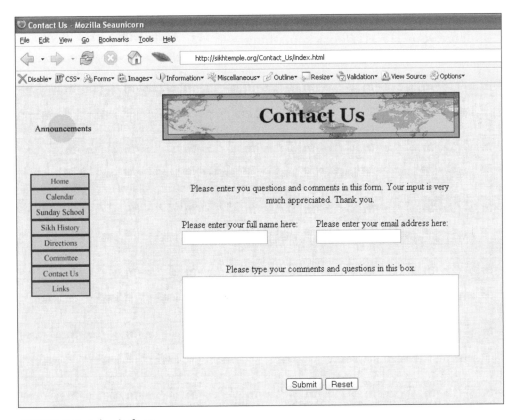

FIGURE 6.9 *A basic form.*

This is the most common form you'll see. It has a few text boxes and some selection boxes, and at the bottom of the page there's a Submit button.

But still, what's a form? It's just a bunch of controls that allow the user to enter information on a page. The form then sends the information to an external script for processing.

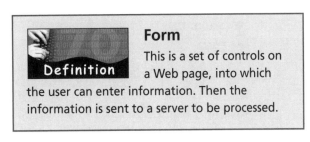

Form
This is a set of controls on a Web page, into which the user can enter information. Then the information is sent to a server to be processed.

Before I show you all of the controls, I want to show you how to set up a basic form in HTML. You need to use the `<FORM>` tag, which tells the Web browser that a form is being defined. There are a lot of attributes to `<FORM>`, but we'll go over them later.

When you're starting a form, make sure your HTML looks something like this.

```
<FORM>
<!-- Controls -->
</FORM>
```

Tag—<FORM></FORM>

This tells the browser that a form is about to be created, and it also explains what action the form will take.

note

If you use the <FORM> tag by itself, nothing will happen. You need to have an action defined, so that the tag does some work. We'll get to actions a little later in the chapter, because they're a bit complex.

To create a control, you need to use the <INPUT> tag. It's a little bit different, because it can be any one of the controls. You define what it is by using the TYPE attribute.

Tag—<INPUT>

This tells the browser which control should be created within the form and what it should do.

So what are the different types of controls on a page? Let's go over the most common ones.

Buttons

Buttons are used on most forms. The user clicks a button to tell the Web site when he's done with the form and ready to submit the information. Actually, there are two types of buttons we'll be talking about in this book:

❖ Submit

❖ Reset

(There's also the Push button, but it isn't that important.) Pretty simple, eh? Take a look at Figure 6.10 to see what they look like. (This is WDFT06-07.html on the companion Web site.)

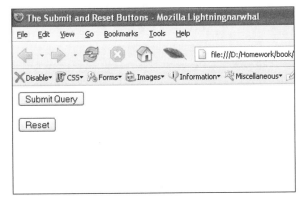

FIGURE 6.10 *Buttons on a form.*

As you can see, there are a couple of buttons on this page. Let's look at the code that created them:

```
<HTML>

<HEAD>
<TITLE>The Submit and Reset Buttons</TITLE>
</HEAD>

<BODY>
<FORM>
<INPUT TYPE=submit>
<P>
<INPUT TYPE=reset>
</FORM>

</BODY>
</HTML>
```

The most important part is the <INPUT> tag in the <BODY> section. How did I get the labels to say Submit Query and Reset? Those are the default values for the Submit button and the Reset button. You can change them, though.

For instance, let's say you want to make the buttons a little different. You could do something like this:

```
<INPUT TYPE=submit VALUE="Whasssup" >
<P>
<INPUT TYPE=reset VALUE="Keepin it real">
```

Given that these are catchphrases from the '90s, feel free to adjust them to suit your needs. Figure 6.11 shows you the Web page with the updated buttons. (This is WDFT06-08.html on the companion Web site.)

Now, before we move on, I want to tell you one thing. With all `<INPUT>` types, you need to use the NAME attribute. This gives each of the controls a hidden name so that you can identify it later,

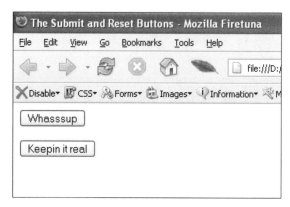

FIGURE 6.11 *New buttons on a form.*

when you want to see what the user has typed. Typically, you don't need names for the buttons because they don't handle any information, but let me show you how it works anyway:

```
<INPUT TYPE=submit VALUE="Whasssup" NAME="submitbutton">
```

Pretty easy, right? This makes a big difference later when the form is submitted, and it doesn't change the look of the actual button in any way.

When you click on the Reset button, everything else in the form reverts to its default value. So, you might use it if you want to allow the user to clear their entries in the form.

There are a few more attributes that relate to buttons, but they also go with everything else on the form, so we'll discuss them later in the chapter.

Text and Password Boxes

You'll probably be using text boxes an awful lot when you use forms. They're pretty common, since it's almost obligatory to allow the user to write out something in text format. Adding a text box to your page is almost as easy as adding a button, except that it's required to have a NAME attribute. Let's take a look at using the <INPUT> tag to make a text box:

```
<INPUT TYPE=text NAME=textboxone>
```

This creates a blank text box called textboxone. Figure 6.12 shows what it looks like. (This is WDFT06-09.html on the companion Web site.)

That's kind of boring, huh? It's just a rectangle! Of course, once you type something into it, the text box becomes a whole lot more.

In fact, you can change what it says by default. For example, let's say you want a text box that says, "My name is." To do this, simply change the value:

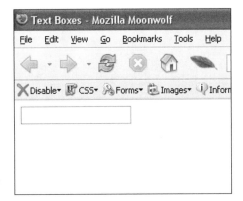

FIGURE 6.12 *A text box.*

```
<INPUT TYPE=text NAME=textboxone VALUE="My name is">
```

This changes the text that appears by default in the text box. This page is WDFT06-10.html on the companion Web site.

> **note** Keep in mind that when you set any of the controls to a default value, the new value in the control will be replaced with the default value when the Reset button is clicked. So for example, if the user types "John" in the text box and then clicks Reset, "My name is" is in the text box. If you don't give it a default value, it will be blank.

What's a password box? It's exactly the same as a text box, except the characters that the user types in aren't shown onscreen. They're replaced with dots or asterisks, so that the password is shielded from outside viewers. Check out Figure 6.13, which shows what the same text looks like in a text box versus a password box. (This is WDFT06-11.html on the companion Web site.)

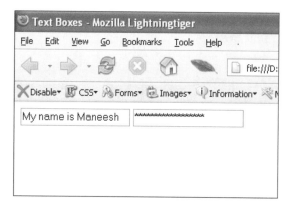

FIGURE 6.13 *A text box versus a password box.*

Both of these text boxes contain the same text, but one is hidden while the other is not. Use this for sensitive information, like passwords or Social Security Numbers (although I don't know why you would need anybody's SSN).

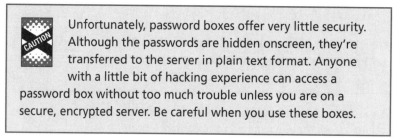

Unfortunately, password boxes offer very little security. Although the passwords are hidden onscreen, they're transferred to the server in plain text format. Anyone with a little bit of hacking experience can access a password box without too much trouble unless you are on a secure, encrypted server. Be careful when you use these boxes.

Let's look at the code that made this happen:

```
<HTML>

<HEAD>
<TITLE>Text Boxes vs. Password Boxes</TITLE>
</HEAD>

<BODY>
<FORM>
<INPUT TYPE=text NAME=textboxone>
<INPUT TYPE=password NAME=textboxtwo>
</FORM>
```

```
</BODY>
</HTML>
```

Not too shabby, eh? The only difference between text boxes and password boxes is the type, which is `password` rather than `text`.

> Password boxes look different in Mozilla Firefox than in Internet Explorer. Figure 6.13 shows a password box in Firefox, but in Internet Explorer, the password characters are dots rather than asterisks. Open it up in IE and take a look!

There's another type of text box that we should go over. This is called the text area, and it's a large box that allows the writing of large comments. You use text areas when you want the user to submit comments or long questions.

Text areas are different from other controls because they don't use the `<INPUT>` tag. Instead, they use the `<TEXTAREA></TEXTAREA>` tag.

> **Tag—`<TEXTAREA></TEXTAREA>`**
> This creates an elongated text box that allows the user to type in lengthy comments.

You can use a few attributes to define the size of the text box. A common size is 10 rows by 40 columns. To create a text box this size, use the following line of code:

```
<TEXTAREA name=comments
ROWS=10 COLS=40>
</TEXTAREA>
```

This will create a text area that looks like Figure 6.14, with a little bit of added text. (This is WDFT06-12.html on the companion Web site.)

Remember that you need to keep it within the `<FORM></FORM>` tag.

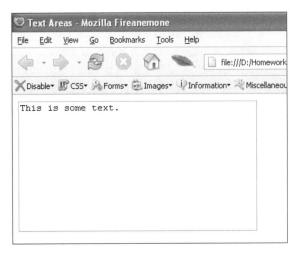

FIGURE 6.14 *A text area.*

By the way, you can give the text area some default text. When the page loads, there will already be some text in the box. To do this, just add the desired text within the `<TEXTAREA></TEXTAREA>` tag:

```
<TEXTAREA name=comments ROWS=10 COLS=40>
This is default text.
</TEXTAREA>
```

"This is default text" will now appear in the text area. You might use default text to tell the visitor to "Type your feedback here," for instance.

Next up, check boxes and radio buttons.

Check boxes and Radio Buttons

Check boxes and radio buttons differ from all of the controls we've discussed so far. They offer only a set number of choices, rather than allowing the user to enter anything he wants. You can list a bunch of options and let the user choose which ones to accept by clicking on a check box or radio button.

What's the difference between a check box and a radio button? Well, they're different shapes. A check box is square and a radio button is circular. Besides that, a radio button allows you to choose only one option out of a set, while a check box allows you to select as many as you want.

You might use a radio button when you want the user to choose something like an age group, a time zone, or anything else that can be only one answer. You use a check box for things like the user's interests, where there can be more than one answer.

What do these look like? Figure 6.15 shows you the difference between radio buttons and check boxes. (This is WDFT06-13.html on the companion Web site.)

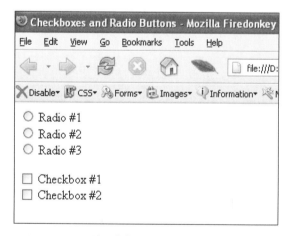

FIGURE 6.15 *Check boxes and radio buttons.*

Pretty simple? Well, the code is a bit more complex:

```
<FORM>
<INPUT TYPE=radio NAME=radioselection VALUE=radio1>Radio #1
<BR>
<INPUT TYPE=radio NAME=radioselection VALUE=radio2>Radio #2
<BR>
<INPUT TYPE=radio NAME=radioselection VALUE=radio3>Radio #3

<P>
<INPUT TYPE=checkbox NAME=checkboxselection VALUE=check1>Checkbox #1
<BR>
<INPUT TYPE=checkbox NAME=checkboxselection VALUE=check2>Checkbox #2
</FORM>
```

Once again, I used the `<INPUT>` tag to create the items, but this time they all have a few more required attributes. First of all, `NAME` is required. Here's the tricky part: For related radio buttons and check boxes, the `NAME` *needs* to be the same. Otherwise, the user can select more than one of the radio buttons, and the results won't mean anything.

Also, each `<INPUT>` tag needs a `VALUE` attribute. This attribute is passed to the server when the form is submitted, and it tells the server which choice was selected. `VALUE` should be different for each radio button and check box.

> **tip** Sometimes, you may want a box to be checked by default. This is especially common with radio buttons. If you don't check an item by default, the user can simply leave it blank. To make an item checked, simply add the `CHECKED` attribute to the `<INPUT>` tag. It doesn't need to be equal to anything. Your tag will look something like this:
>
>   <INPUT TYPE=radio CHECKED> Radio
>
> Don't forget the `NAME` and `VALUE` tags!

Note that the `VALUE` tag doesn't display anything on the screen. To add a name to the control, as with Radio #1 and Checkbox #2, you need to use basic HTML text. Just add the name after the end of the `<INPUT>` tag, and it will appear after the radio button.

Let's move on to the last two controls: file select and hidden.

File Select and Hidden Controls

The file select control allows the user to upload files to you. You won't use it very often, but I figured you'd want to see it anyway.

To use the file select control, simply use the `<INPUT>` tag with the `TYPE` attribute set to `file`. A box like the one in Figure 6.16 will appear. (This is WDFT06-14.html on the companion Web site.)

The Browse button appears automatically. When you click it, a file selection window pops up and you can choose the file.

The last type of control I want to discuss is the hidden control, which allows you to send hidden information in the form. This is useful when you have different forms on the same site, and you want to delineate

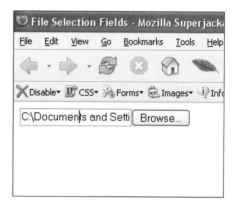

FIGURE 6.16 *File selection control.*

between them. In addition, many methods of sending data through forms require you to use some hidden information so that an action can occur. For example, you might add a hidden control called `email`, and the results of the form will be sent to the specified e-mail address.

To create a hidden control, use something like this:

```
<INPUT TYPE=hidden NAME=email VALUE="maneesh@maneeshsethi.com">
```

As you can see, you use `NAME`, `TYPE`, and `VALUE`, just as in the other `<INPUT>` tags.

All right! Now you know about all of the controls on forms. Let's talk about how to use them.

Submitting Forms

Unfortunately, submitting forms is a little more complex than creating them. It requires a separate programming language to send the form through the system. The good news is that you can find a lot of these scripts for free online. Check out sites such as bignosebird.com and scriptarchive.com for free scripts.

I created a short PHP script for my Web site that allows a form to be submitted to any e-mail address. The file is called sendmail.php on the companion Web site, and it looks something like this:

```
<?
  $from = $_REQUEST['from'] ;
  $recipient = $_REQUEST['recipient'] ;

  mail( "$recipient", "Subscribe to ManeeshSethi.com - WDFT",
   "From: $from" );
  header( "Location: thankyou.html" );
?>
```

As you can see, this doesn't look very similar to HTML. You need to look at the top, where it says 'from' and 'recipient'. These are simply controls on the form. On my Web site, the from control is a text box where the user types in his e-mail address, and the recipient control is a hidden control that has my e-mail address as its value. When the user types in his e-mail address and clicks Submit, an e-mail is sent to the recipient with the user's e-mail address as its body.

You need to set up a Web server in order to use PHP scripts, so you won't be able to adjust this script unless you have access to a PHP server.

Let me show you how you get a script working. The first thing you need to do is tell the form which script it will use by adding some attributes to the <FORM></FORM> tag:

```
<FORM NAME="form1" ACTION="http://www.maneeshsethi.com/sendmail.php"
METHOD="post">
```

First, you create a form and give it a name. Then, make an ACTION attribute and set it equal to the script you want to use. If you create your own script on your Web site, you can set the form to that script. Lastly, set the METHOD to post. There are two types of METHOD attributes, get and post. Typically, get is used with database applications and post is used with submitted forms. You should use post in most cases.

Now that you've set up the form, you just need to create the controls. WDFT06-15.html shows the code used to create the form:

```
<HTML>

<HEAD>
```

```
<TITLE>Setting Up a Form</TITLE>
</HEAD>

<BODY>
<FORM NAME=form1 ACTION=http://www.maneeshsethi.com/sendmailwdft.php
METHOD=POST>
<INPUT TYPE=text NAME=from>
<INPUT TYPE=hidden NAME=recipient VALUE=maneesh@maneeshsethi.com>
<INPUT TYPE=submit>
</FORM>

</BODY>
</HTML>
```

All you have to do is type in your e-mail address, and it will send your address to me. If you change the VALUE to your own e-mail address, it will send your own address to you! Look at Figure 6.17 to see what this page looks like. (This is WDFT06-15.html on the companion Web site.)

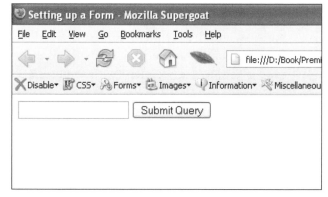

FIGURE 6.17 *Using forms.*

> **note** Note that immediately after you submit the form, you're taken to the Thank You page on www.maneeshsethi.com. That's because the PHP file is set up to direct you there. This is your chance to subscribe to ManeeshSethi.com! Just type in your e-mail address, and you'll be subscribed to the site automatically. If you try this out, you will get a response in a couple of days telling you that you are subscribed to www.maneeshsethi.com, and you can cancel if you decide not to subscribe.

Creating forms in Nvu is also a little difficult to do, especially with all of the different controls. Let's make a simple one using Nvu. First of all, make sure the program is open on your computer.

See the Form button on the main task bar? Click the little arrow next to it. A window pops up, as shown in Figure 6.18.

This menu allows you to access all of the form creation utilities. The first thing you need to do is define the form. Select Define Form. A box pops up that allows you to choose the NAME, ACTION, and METHOD attributes. After that, the outline of a form is drawn on the screen.

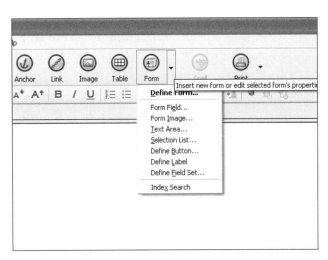

FIGURE 6.18 *Creating a form in Nvu.*

To create controls, just make sure that the cursor is within the outline of the form. Then, click on the arrow next to the Form button to create the controls.

There are a lot of options and controls that you can create in the menu. Usually, you'll use the Form Field option, which allows you to create any of the controls we've discussed. Figure 6.19 shows the Form Field Properties box.

Click the arrow next to the Text field. The drop-down menu shows all of the controls.

Using this tool, you can create all of the controls in the form, and you can assign them names and initial values. Nvu also supports some really cool features, like selection boxes, which display a list of items and allow the user to select one of them. To create a selection box, just click on the Form arrow and choose Selection List.

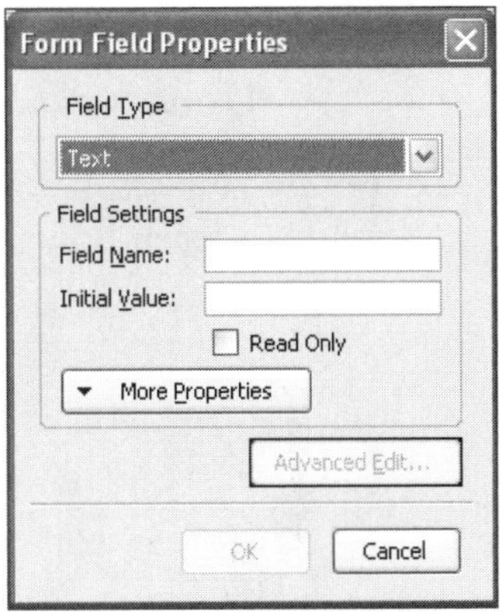

FIGURE 6.19 *The Form Field Properties box in Nvu.*

Nvu can save you a lot of time creating forms, but remember that it creates ugly code and hurts reusability. Only use it when the function you want will take an inordinate amount of time to code by hand.

Well, that's just about it for forms. You can learn how to script your own tools by learning PHP or Perl. If you use these languages or download scripts written in them, you'll be able to extend your form to allow you to submit anything you want.

If you have any questions about forms or want some help extending your form to fit your needs, e-mail me at maneesh@maneeshsethi.com and I'll be glad to help you.

Summary

Whew, that was a really long chapter. We sure did learn a lot though, huh?

In this chapter, you learned about the following:

- ❖ Hyperlinks
- ❖ Bullet lists
- ❖ Numbered lists
- ❖ Definition lists
- ❖ Creating forms
- ❖ Creating controls in forms
- ❖ Sending data through forms
- ❖ Using Nvu to simplify labor

I hope you enjoyed this chapter, because the next one will wrap up Part 2. Get ready to learn how to create tables and multimedia!

Chapter 7
Tables and Multimedia

Welcome back! We're nearing the end of Part 2. After just one more chapter, you'll put all that you've learned so far into creating actual Web pages. But first, you need to learn about tables and multimedia.

Tables and multimedia are both integral parts of today's Web design. Almost all Web sites use tables. They give a site structure and form, rather than just presenting a glut of information. In addition, with the increase of bandwidth and computing power in the past few years, multimedia is a formidable presence on the Web. Multimedia helps to expand and define your Web site, and it allows you to present your information in ways that you couldn't have done only a few years ago.

Let's get to the crux of the chapter: tables.

Tables

We went over tables briefly in Chapter 3, but let's refresh your memory: A table organizes information in an easy-to-understand manner. Table 7.1 shows an example of a simple table.

Table 7.1 Good Sites on the Internet

Site	Description
www.ebay.com	A site where you can buy and sell items.
www.cnn.com	An excellent news site.
www.maneeshsethi.com	The best site in the world.

See how this organizes the data? That's what tables do. However, organizing data isn't the only function they serve.

The biggest reason to use a table is because it allows you to add structure to a Web page. Using tables, you can create navigation bars and header sections, and you can organize your Web page so it isn't, well, boring.

Let me tell you a secret: The way to achieve good design is through asymmetry. What is asymmetry? It's the opposite of *symmetry*, which is when everything is equal on both sides, such as the left half of the page being balanced with the right side. Look at Figure 7.1 for an example.

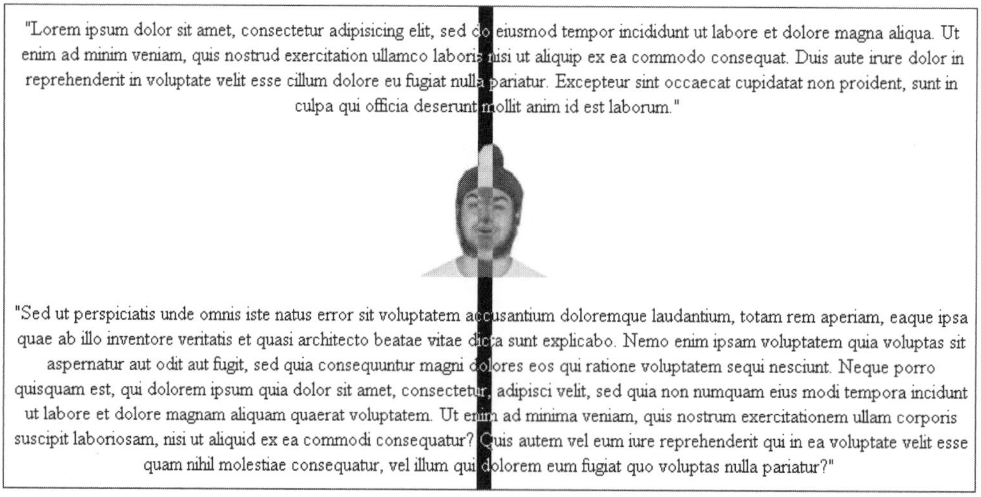

"Lorem ipsum dolor sit amet, consectetur adipisicing elit, sed do eiusmod tempor incididunt ut labore et dolore magna aliqua. Ut enim ad minim veniam, quis nostrud exercitation ullamco laboris nisi ut aliquip ex ea commodo consequat. Duis aute irure dolor in reprehenderit in voluptate velit esse cillum dolore eu fugiat nulla pariatur. Excepteur sint occaecat cupidatat non proident, sunt in culpa qui officia deserunt mollit anim id est laborum."

"Sed ut perspiciatis unde omnis iste natus error sit voluptatem accusantium doloremque laudantium, totam rem aperiam, eaque ipsa quae ab illo inventore veritatis et quasi architecto beatae vitae dicta sunt explicabo. Nemo enim ipsam voluptatem quia voluptas sit aspernatur aut odit aut fugit, sed quia consequuntur magni dolores eos qui ratione voluptatem sequi nesciunt. Neque porro quisquam est, qui dolorem ipsum quia dolor sit amet, consectetur, adipisci velit, sed quia non numquam eius modi tempora incidunt ut labore et dolore magnam aliquam quaerat voluptatem. Ut enim ad minima veniam, quis nostrum exercitationem ullam corporis suscipit laboriosam, nisi ut aliquid ex ea commodi consequatur? Quis autem vel eum iure reprehenderit qui in ea voluptate velit esse quam nihil molestiae consequatur, vel illum qui dolorem eum fugiat quo voluptas nulla pariatur?"

FIGURE 7.1 *Symmetry in action.*

Not too fun to read, huh? Sure, it's not interesting in the first place because it's in Latin, but I bet the first thing you said when you saw it was, "This is too boring for me to read! It should be split up a little."

Splitting up a page is the job of tables. They let you move items around and make certain parts of the page stand out. This makes the page much more pleasing to the eye.

Figure 7.2 shows the same page, only with *asymmetry*.

See the difference? The page is more weighted to the left. If you then add more images, colors, and elements to the page, the asymmetry makes a big difference.

Now that you understand what tables can do for your page, let's find out how you can make them work. First of all, we'll discuss how to use tables to organize simple data.

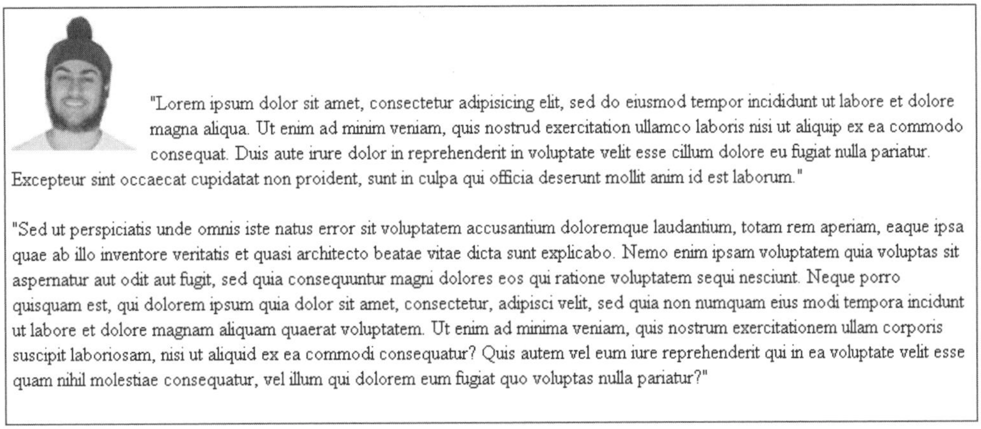

"Lorem ipsum dolor sit amet, consectetur adipisicing elit, sed do eiusmod tempor incididunt ut labore et dolore magna aliqua. Ut enim ad minim veniam, quis nostrud exercitation ullamco laboris nisi ut aliquip ex ea commodo consequat. Duis aute irure dolor in reprehenderit in voluptate velit esse cillum dolore eu fugiat nulla pariatur. Excepteur sint occaecat cupidatat non proident, sunt in culpa qui officia deserunt mollit anim id est laborum."

"Sed ut perspiciatis unde omnis iste natus error sit voluptatem accusantium doloremque laudantium, totam rem aperiam, eaque ipsa quae ab illo inventore veritatis et quasi architecto beatae vitae dicta sunt explicabo. Nemo enim ipsam voluptatem quia voluptas sit aspernatur aut odit aut fugit, sed quia consequuntur magni dolores eos qui ratione voluptatem sequi nesciunt. Neque porro quisquam est, qui dolorem ipsum quia dolor sit amet, consectetur, adipisci velit, sed quia non numquam eius modi tempora incidunt ut labore et dolore magnam aliquam quaerat voluptatem. Ut enim ad minima veniam, quis nostrum exercitationem ullam corporis suscipit laboriosam, nisi ut aliquid ex ea commodi consequatur? Quis autem vel eum iure reprehenderit qui in ea voluptate velit esse quam nihil molestiae consequatur, vel illum qui dolorem eum fugiat quo voluptas nulla pariatur?"

FIGURE 7.2 *Asymmetry in (better) action.*

Creating Basic Tables

Setting up tables isn't too bad. You just need to add a few more tags to your already substantial portfolio.

The first tag you need to learn is the `<TABLE></TABLE>` tag. This is used to create the outline for the table. Without it, the rest of this section is worthless!

> **Tag—`<TABLE></TABLE>`**
> This encloses the entire table and allows the browser to display the row and column tags.

The `<TABLE></TABLE>` tag is just like the `<FORM></FORM>` tag. Although both will function without any attributes, they can do much more *with* attributes. Using attributes in `<TABLE></TABLE>` allows you to extend the capabilities of the table.

The first attribute you can use is `ALIGN`. This tag lets you choose where the table will appear on the page. You can choose either `left`, `center`, or `right` as your value. If you do not use `ALIGN`, the table will default to being aligned left. Figure 7.3 shows a table that is aligned to the right. (This is WDFT07-01.html on the companion Web site.)

FIGURE 7.3 *Right-aligned table.*

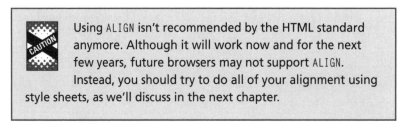

Using `ALIGN` isn't recommended by the HTML standard anymore. Although it will work now and for the next few years, future browsers may not support `ALIGN`. Instead, you should try to do all of your alignment using style sheets, as we'll discuss in the next chapter.

The second and third attributes, `WIDTH` and `HEIGHT`, modify the size of the table. If you do not use these attributes, a table will be the smallest necessary size to fit the cells within it. `WIDTH` and `HEIGHT` let you choose exactly how these cells will look on the page.

You can express `WIDTH` and `HEIGHT` as either percentages or measured in pixels. Using percentages always makes the table appear the same length no matter what the viewer's resolution is, but it may make some images look distorted. Using pixels allows for a more exact definition of the item's size.

WHEN SHOULD I USE PERCENTAGES RATHER THAN PIXEL SIZE?

I almost always use pixel sizes rather than percentages, so that the images will appear correctly no matter the resolution of the user's computer. The unfortunate side effect is that if your table is wider or longer than the viewer's browser, he'll have to scroll around to see the image.

Because of this, I recommend that you never make a table more than 800 pixels wide. If you can, try to keep it less than 600 pixels tall as well, but this is less important than keeping it less than 800 pixels wide.

You can use percentages if your table has few or no images, and if you want to make sure the text appears on one screen for all viewers.

Let's look at how to make the table from Figure 7.3 take up the entire browser by making the WIDTH 100%. Figure 7.4 shows what happens. (This is WDFT07-02.html on the companion Web site.)

It's a little ugly, huh? It's stretched out of shape. However, for other types of tables, it makes more sense to stretch them the full length of the browser.

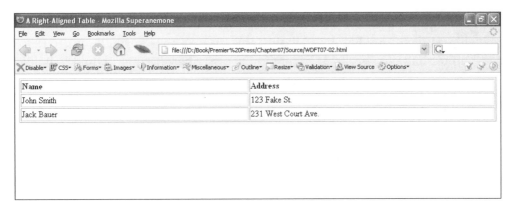

FIGURE 7.4 *A 100% wide table.*

Let's look at the code for this table:

```
<TABLE ALIGN=right BORDER=1 WIDTH=100%>
<TR><TH ALIGN=left> Name
<TH ALIGN=left> Address


<TR><TD>John Smith
<TD>123 Fake St.


<TR><TD>Jack Bauer
<TD>231 West Court Ave.


</TABLE>
```

Don't worry about all the `<TR>`s and `<TD>`s. We'll be going over them soon. Just take a look at the `<TABLE></TABLE>` tag.

First of all, notice that the `ALIGN` tag is set to the right. In this case, the alignment makes no difference because the table takes up 100% of the screen. Even if it were aligned as `center` or `left`, the table would look the same because `WIDTH` is 100%. But if `WIDTH` were anything else, the alignment would change.

The next tag is another one of `TABLE`'s attributes: `BORDER`. This tag creates that little border around each cell in the table. In many cases, you'll set `BORDER` to 0, but in this table it's set to 1. Figure 7.5 shows what the table would look like without any borders. (This is WDFT07-03.html on the companion Web site.)

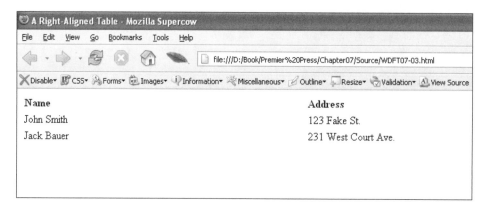

FIGURE 7.5 *A table without borders.*

The last attribute is WIDTH. In this case, the table is the exact width of the browser because it's set to 100%.

Table 7.2 shows all of the attributes we've discussed for the <TABLE></TABLE> tag.

Table 7.2 <TABLE> Attributes

Tag	Description
BORDER	Defines the thickness of the border around each cell. 0 by default.
ALIGN	Aligns the table to either the right, left, or center. Left by default.
WIDTH	Describes the width of the table in either percentages or pixels.
HEIGHT	Describes the height of the table in either percentages or pixels.

Now let's learn how to create table rows, columns, and cells.

Creating Table Cells

Creating table cells isn't much harder than creating the table in the first place. There are three new tags that go into the creation of cells: <TR>, <TD>, and <TH>. These tags do not require closing tags, but they are acceptable. You can use <TR></TR>, but make sure you stay consistent. In this book, I use closing tags only when the document was made with Nvu.

The first tag, <TR>, creates a new row of items. You should use this in your table every time you want to create a new row of items.

> **Tag—<TR>**
> This creates a new row in a table.

The <TD> tag creates a new cell within the row. If you have three <TD> tags within one <TR> tag, you'll have a three-column table.

> **Tag—<TD>**
> This creates a new data cell in a table.

Let's look at the table from WDFT07-02.html:

```
<TR>
<TH ALIGN=left> Name
<TH ALIGN=left> Address
```

```
<TR>
<TD> John Smith
<TD> 123 Fake St.


<TR>
<TD> Jack Bauer
<TD> 231 West Court Ave.
```

As you can see, because there are three `<TR>` tags, there are three rows. Within the first row, you notice another tag, the `<TH>` tag. This is a table header tag. The main difference is that the word is boldfaced and centered. I wanted it to be left-aligned, so I set `ALIGN` to the left.

After the first row, there are two more rows that have information that's displayed in the table. Now, what if you want to add a title to the table?

Figure 7.6 shows what happens if you try to create a title in the table using the `<TR>` tag. (This is WDFT07-04.html on the companion Web site.)

> ### Tag—`<TH>`
> This creates a new header tag in a table.

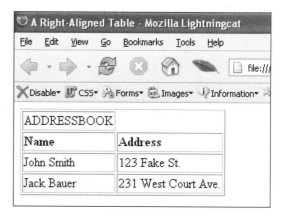

FIGURE 7.6 *A messed-up title.*

 I changed the code from WDFT07-02.html a little in the following examples. The main differences are that I aligned the table to the left and gave it a smaller width.

That doesn't look very good. You want that title to span both columns, so that it really looks like a title. Fortunately, HTML provides a method to do this. Set the COLSPAN attribute equal to the number of columns. Figure 7.7 shows how it looks onscreen. (This is WDFT07-05.html on the companion Web site.)

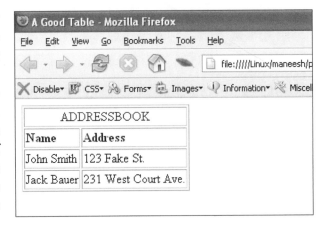

FIGURE 7.7 *A better title.*

You can also span multiple rows with ROWSPAN.

What happens if the cell is too large and you want to align the text to the top or bottom of the cell? Fortunately, you can set the VALIGN attribute to top, center, or bottom to align the text vertically.

Spacing and the Background of Tables

There are a few more attributes that allow you to change the spacing of cells and the background of tables. These attributes allow you to make your tables even better.

For spacing, you can use the CELLSPACING and CELLPADDING attributes. The CELLSPACING attribute sets an amount of space in pixels between the table borders and cells. Compare Figure 7.8, which uses CELLSPACING (and is WDFT07-06.html on the companion Web site), with Figure 7.7.

The difference is that the distance from the border to the cell has been enlarged. Figure 7.9 shows what happens when you use CELLPADDING instead. (This is WDFT07-07.html on the companion Web site.)

The major difference in CELLPADDING is that the distance from the border to the data in the cell has been expanded.

These new attributes allow you to expand your tables and make them look more pleasing to the eye. Experiment with these attributes until your table looks good and does its job of displaying data well.

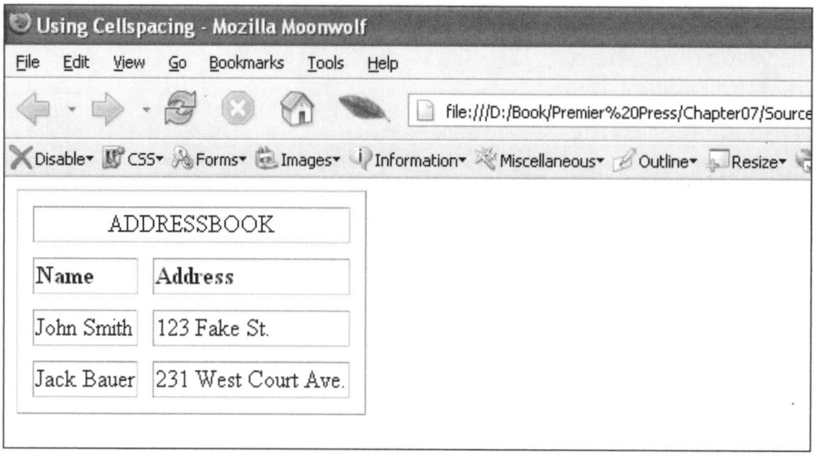

FIGURE 7.8 *Using CELLSPACING.*

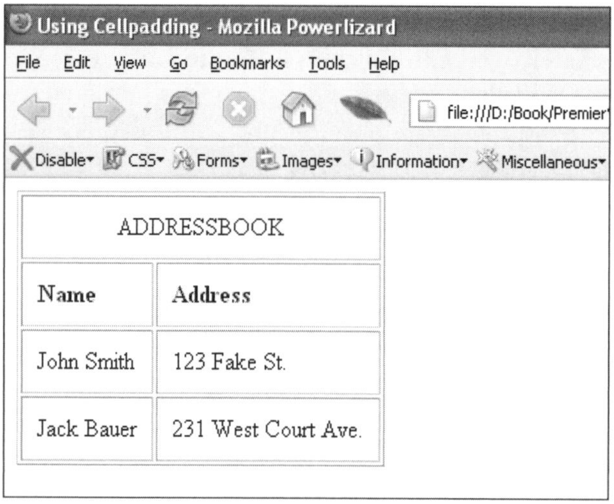

FIGURE 7.9 *Using CELLPADDING.*

You can also add a different background color to each cell or to the entire table. You can use either color names or the RGB values that we went over earlier. Just add the BGCOLOR attribute to the <TD> or <TABLE> tags.

Figure 7.10 shows how I added color to the entire table as well as to an individual cell. The table is a light shade of gray, while the "John Smith" cell is red. (This is WDFT07-08.html on the companion Web site.)

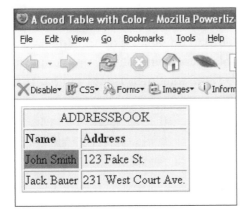

FIGURE 7.10 *Using background colors.*

Let's look at the HTML that made this:

```
<TABLE BORDER=1 BGCOLOR=#EEEEEE>
<TR><TD COLSPAN=2 ALIGN=center>ADDRESSBOOK

<TR>
<TH ALIGN=left> Name
<TH ALIGN=left> Address

<TR> <TD BGCOLOR=red> John Smith
<TD> 123 Fake St.


<TR> <TD> Jack Bauer
<TD> 231 West Court Ave.


</TABLE>
```

Notice that there are two tags that use `BGCOLOR`, the `<TABLE>` tag and the `<TD>` tag before "John Smith." As you can see, the entire table is set to #EEEEEE, which is a very light shade of gray. The John Smith cell, however, is set to red. The main thing to notice is that the cell color overrides the color of the entire table. If you set the color of a cell, the color of the table doesn't matter.

Going Easy: Using Nvu for Tables

Creating tables with Nvu is a little easier than doing it by hand. However, unlike forms, Nvu doesn't have most of its table options in one popup menu. Instead, you need to do a lot of the editing with right-click menus and toolbar menus.

To create the outline for the table, click the Table tool on the main toolbar. Figure 7.11 shows the window that pops up.

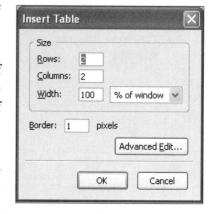

In this window, you can choose the number of rows and columns, as well as the size. Click the Advanced Edit button to edit a number of options, including CELLSPACING, CELLPADDING, and BORDER.

After you've created the table, you can enter data into the columns and rows you've created. The table menu at the top of the screen allows you to select, edit, and delete items from your table.

FIGURE 7.11 *The Insert Table window.*

If you want to merge cells, highlight the rows you want to merge, right-click, and select Merge Cells. You can split cells in the same way.

You can do a lot more with tables in Nvu. Just use the menus to try different things!

That's about it for tables. Let's learn a little about Internet multimedia.

Multimedia in Web Pages

A panda walks into a bar. He sits down and orders some food. After eating, he gets up, shoots a drunk, and exits the bar. The bartender runs after him and asks him why he did it. The panda says, "Look up 'panda' in the dictionary." The man goes back and gets his dictionary, looks the word up, and reads, "Panda. Large black-and-white bear-like mammal, native to China. Eats, shoots and leaves."

What can multimedia do for you? Well, if you use sound rather than text, you get rid of punctuation errors that cause problems like that! But in any case, multimedia will really help you expand everything you do on your Web pages.

What is multimedia? It's anything you put on your page beyond text and graphics. That includes music, video, sound, animation, and everything else. In this section, you'll learn how to add sound and video to your page.

The following is important to remember: Just because you *can* add multimedia doesn't mean you *should*. In most cases, you shouldn't have video or music on your page. Background music can interfere with the user's ability to understand what they're reading, or even worse, could make them give up and leave. I recommend avoiding background music as much as possible.

Maxim # 7
"Be careful with multimedia.
Especially when it's annoying."

On the other hand, using sound on some pages could work. For example, a sound file that reads a hard-to-pronounce word could be very useful.

The first (and typically the best) way to use audio on a page is through a simple hyperlink. Just create a normal link to your sound file and let the user download it if they want. For example, go to the companion Web site and listen to wdft.wav, an introductory sound file that I created for this book. You should be able to listen to it with whatever music program you have on your computer.

Now, let's say you want to put that sound on your Web site. The best way is to let the user click on a link and download the file. Here's the code to do this:

```
<HTML>
<HEAD>
<TITLE>Sound as a Hyperlink</TITLE>
</HEAD>

<BODY>

<P>Welcome to my Web Design for Teens page.
<P>Would you like to be introduced by me personally? If so, <A
HREF="wdft.wav">click here to download the sound clip!</A>

</BODY>
</HTML>
```

Figure 7.12 shows how this looks onscreen. (This is WDFT07-09.html on the companion Web site.)

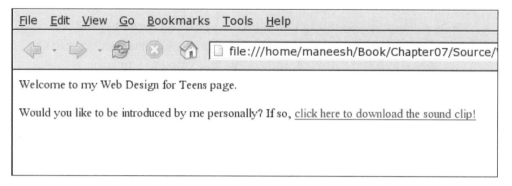

FIGURE 7.12 *Hyperlinked sounds.*

As you can see, this is a simple HTML document with a simple hyperlink. When the user clicks on the link, he can listen to the file on his default sound player. In many browsers, the item will load without even prompting the user, so that the sound plays almost instantaneously!

Now that you know how to link to a sound file, let me show you something a little more complex. Let's learn how to make the browser play a sound file automatically.

Remember Maxim #7, about being careful with multimedia? When you set a sound file to be played automatically, it can be pretty annoying to the user. You need to weigh the benefits of playing the file with the negatives of ruining the user's Web browsing.

Now that you've been cautioned, let's do this. There are two methods, but one of them works only in Internet Explorer. The IE way uses the `<BGSOUND></BGSOUND>` tag. In addition, you can use a couple of the attributes that are summarized in Table 7.3.

> **Tag—`<BGSOUND></BGSOUND>`**
> This allows you to play background sound files in Internet Explorer.

Table 7.3—`<BGSOUND>` Attributes

Site	Description
SRC	The filename of the sound file (can be relative to the file or absolute).
LOOP	The number of times you want it to play. 0 = 1 time, -1 = an infinite number of times.
BALANCE	The amount of sound that's played on the left speaker vs. the right speaker. -10,000 is all the way to the left, 0 is in the center, 10,000 is all the way to the right.
VOLUME	Volume of the speakers. Between -10,000 and 0, with 0 being full volume.

Keep in mind that `<BGSOUND></BGSOUND>` only works in Internet Explorer. This means that anyone who uses a different browser (like me!) won't be able to hear the sound. This may be a blessing on pages where the background sound is incredibly annoying, but you still shouldn't use `<BGSOUND></BGSOUND>` unless you have a very good reason.

The second method of playing sound uses the `<EMBED>` tag. The really cool thing about this tag is that it inserts a small window that lets the user control the sound. The user can choose whether to play it or not, and he doesn't need to download the file to his computer or anything. Figure 7.13 shows what this browser-embedded tool looks like.

Tag—`<EMBED></EMBED>`
This allows you to embed other types of files directly into a page, including both sound and video.

FIGURE 7.13 *Inline sounds using <EMBED>.*

Note that Figure 7.13 was taken from a computer running Internet Explorer with Windows Media Player 9 installed. The image may look different depending on the program being run, and on some other browsers, it may not run at all without a downloaded plug-in.

Pretty cool, eh? The ⟨EMBED⟩ tag takes care of all the work for you.

Now, one problem is that ⟨EMBED⟩ is supported differently by different browsers. Some browsers accept more tags than others do. For that reason, I'm going to show you only the tags that work on *all* browsers that use ⟨EMBED⟩.

The first attribute is SRC. This is just the location of the file you want to play. For example, if you're using the file we used earlier, wdft.wav, SRC would equal wdft.wav. Note that the link must point to the exact location of the sound, so if the location is in "sounds/wdft.wav," your SRC attribute must equal "sounds/wdft.wav."

 I'll be using the phrase "other browsers" a lot in the next few paragraphs. For the most part, "other browsers" means those based on Netscape: Mozilla, Firefox, and of course Netscape itself.

The next two attributes, WIDTH and HEIGHT, are similar to each other. You've seen these attributes waaay too much over the past few chapters, and here they are again. They define the width of the control panel pictured in Figure 7.13. Most people use 144 as their optimal pixel length, so usually it's good to stick with that.

The next attribute, NAME, is pretty common also. Even though it's not strictly necessary, you should probably give your item a name to set it apart in case you ever add more sounds in the future.

You can also choose to make the console invisible! If you would prefer the sound to be played automatically without the user doing anything, set the HID-DEN attribute to "true" (or set it to "false" if you don't).

There are a few more attributes that you should know about. Unfortunately, they don't work exactly the same on Internet Explorer as they do on other browsers, so you need to be careful. The first attribute is LOOP. This works on most browsers other than Internet Explorer. LOOP tells the Web page how many times the sound should repeat. Set it equal to "true" to loop continuously, or to a specific number to make it play a certain number of times.

You can do this same thing with Internet Explorer also, but you need to use the PLAYCOUNT attribute rather than LOOP. Set PLAYCOUNT equal to the number of times you want the item to repeat, just like with LOOP. Unfortunately, you can't use LOOP and PLAYCOUNT at the same time (using LOOP will make it play forever on Internet Explorer), and since many more people use IE than anything else, you will probably stick with PLAYCOUNT for the most part.

The last attribute I want to discuss is AUTOSTART. You should make sure to initialize this tag, because its default is false in Internet Explorer but true in other browsers.

Now let's make a sample sound file. Let's say you want to make an embedded sound section that plays the sound.wav file two times, is not hidden, and starts automatically. The following code shows you how to do it:

```
<BODY>
<!--... intro stuff -->
<EMBED SRC=sound.wav NAME="My Sound" PLAYCOUNT=2 AUTOSTART=true>
<!--... outtro stuff -->
</BODY>
```

I put this <EMBED> to work in WDFT07-10.html. Figure 7.14 shows what it looks like onscreen.

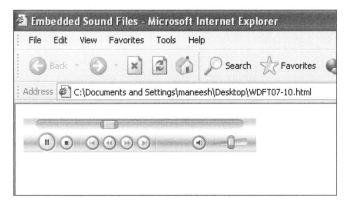

FIGURE 7.14 *Using sounds.*

Before we close out this chapter, I want to teach you about embedding video. Because bandwidth is increasing so rapidly these days, you might want to put some essential video on your Web page, and <EMBED> does the job.

One of the best formats to use for video is Apple Quicktime. It's cross-platform, so no matter what type of computer or operating system the user is running, the file will work as long as the proper plug-in is in use.

So how would you embed an mpeg file? Well, you simply do something like the following:

```
<HTML>
<HEAD>
<TITLE>Embedded Movie</TITLE>
</HEAD>
<BODY>
<EMBED NAME="Movie" SRC="movie.mov" AUTOPLAY=true WIDTH=640 HEIGHT=368>
</BODY>
</HTML>
```

All right! Now you know how to add multimedia to your page.

Summary

One more left until we're done with Part 2.

In this chapter, you learned about:

❖ Tables

❖ Sound

❖ Video

❖ Inserting multimedia into a Web page

Next up is a short primer on Cascading Style Sheets, which are just about the coolest things on the Internet—but are also pretty difficult to learn.

Chapter 8

Cascading Style Sheets

Welcome to the last chapter of Part 2! You're going to learn about Cascading Style Sheets (CSS) in this chapter. CSS is extremely powerful. It allows you to extend everything you've done in HTML and makes it a heck of a lot prettier. However, this functionality comes at a cost. CSS is a little more complex and harder to understand than HTML.

This chapter will discuss the three forms of CSS and how to apply these forms to a Web site. It will also go over the different style attributes that you can use to adjust the style on your page.

What Is CSS?

CSS is one of the strongest methods for Web designers to add style to a Web page. Style sheets control all of the elements of a page, such as the margins, the borders, the font, and the typeface. In addition, you can use CSS to adjust your tables, backgrounds, and link styles. All of these elements are completely configurable within the bounds of style sheets.

Cascading Style Sheets
This is an extension to HTML that allows Web designers to specify styles such as font and color for specific elements of the Web page.

Let's talk about the three types of style sheets:

❖ **Inline:** Using inline style sheets lets you define the style of each element directly within the tag that precedes the word. For example, if you wanted to change the font face of a specific hyperlink to Arial, your tag might look like this: `<A HREF="something.doc" STYLE="font: arial">This is Arial text.</A>`

❖ **Embedded:** Embedded style sheets allow you to define the style for an entire Web page. To define an embedded style sheet, you add the page's style information in the header section of the page (before the `<BODY>` tag). The styles are reflected throughout the page.

❖ **Linked:** The linked style sheet is the strongest of all three forms, because it allows you to define an entire Web site with one style sheet. You create an external document with the suffix .css, such as mypage.css, and you link to the style sheet in the header of your page. All of the styles are loaded directly from that file. Because of this, you can make a simple change in that document, and the changes will be reflected throughout your entire site.

Now that you know the three types, let's learn how to use each one.

Inline Style Sheets

Inline is the easiest style to add to an existing Web page, because all you have to do is insert the style definition into existing tags. You can add this style to most tags that affect text in any way. Usually, if you think that adding an inline style to a specific tag will make a difference, it will.

So, What Is Cascading?

You've been hearing all about these Cascading Style Sheets, but you probably don't even know what those three words mean. "Cascading" means that you have different levels of power in different style sheets—in Web pages, inline is the most powerful, and linked is the least powerful. When you use a linked style sheet, for instance, you might change the font color of all of the paragraph text. But what if you want a specific paragraph to be green, even though the rest of the text is black? Fortunately, inline style sheets are more powerful, overriding the linked style sheets. So, if you ever need something to go against the global linked style sheet, an inline style sheet will allow you to get the effect that you want.

One of the most common tags you might add an inline style to is the `<P>` tag, which defines a new paragraph. If you wanted to make the font of an entire paragraph 12 point Garamond, you might do something like this:

```
<P STYLE="font: 12pt garamond">I am some Garamond text.</a>
```

In this case, the Garamond font is shown on the viewer's computer in 12-point type. However, if the reader's computer doesn't have Garamond installed, this will revert to the default Times New Roman font.

Be careful with the fonts you use. Not everyone's computer has the same fonts, and Apple computers don't always have the same fonts as Windows machines. Stick to the most common fonts: Arial, Verdana, Helvetica, and Times New Roman. Be careful with any other fonts.

There's one way to make sure that the proper font appears on the user's screen: List several fonts with commas between them. The browser will try to use the first font, and if that doesn't work, it will try the second font, and so on. If you wanted some text to be either Verdana, Arial, or Helvetica, you'd write something like this: `<P STYLE= "font-family: verdana, arial, helvetica,sans-serif;>`. (Why did I use `sans-serif`? Because it's a basic font that's installed on every system.)

Let's design a Web page that uses CSS. Figure 8.1 shows you a sample page that adjusts fonts with inline styles. (This is WDFT08-01.html on the companion Web site.)

As you can see, the three different paragraphs have different fonts, sizes, and colors. Although you can do this in pure HTML, using style sheets makes the work a lot more manageable.

Let's take a look at the code that makes this happen:

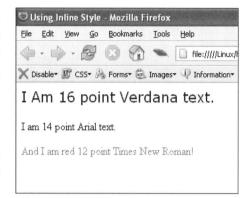

FIGURE 8.1 *Inline style.*

```
<BODY>
<P STYLE="font: 16pt verdana">I Am 16 point Verdana text.
<P STYLE="font 14pt arial">I am 14 point Arial text.
<P STYLE="font: 12pt times new roman; color: red">And I am red 12 point Times
New Roman!
</BODY>
```

You add an attribute to each <P> tag that refers to the style of that paragraph. Within the quotes, write the name of the property you want to edit (font), followed by a colon and then the value of the property.

If you want to edit two different properties within one inline tag, use a semicolon (;) to differentiate between them. In this code, the semicolons in the third paragraph specify that you want to edit both the font and the color.

What if you don't want to edit a whole paragraph, though? Maybe you just want to add a style to one or two words on the page. Fortunately, HTML includes a couple of tags to help you out: <DIV></DIV> and <SPAN></SPAN>. You can wrap either tag around any amount of text you want, and you can add the STYLE attribute to change the style of any text within the tags.

> **Tag—<DIV></DIV>**
> This allows you to align more than one paragraph at a time.

> **Tag—<SPAN></SPAN>**
> This allows you to add style sheets to as much text as necessary.

Remember using the <DIV></DIV> tag to align paragraphs in Chapter 5? This tag lets you edit a bunch of text at the same time. Same thing with <SPAN></SPAN>. You can edit as much text as you want, without having to worry about paragraph breaks or anything like that.

So what's the difference? Well, <DIV></DIV> automatically inserts a line break at the end, and <SPAN></SPAN> doesn't. If you want to change the style of only a few words in a paragraph, you probably want to use <SPAN></SPAN>.

Let's see how this stuff looks in code:

```
<BODY>
Hello, I am regular body text. I am glad you are enjoying reading me, and
<SPAN STYLE="font-size: 14pt">I am larger than</SPAN> the rest of the text.
<P>You might notice that after I finish the emphasized text in this
paragraph, a <DIV STYLE="font-size: 14pt">new line is created</DIV> because
of the DIV tag.
</BODY>
```

Pretty cool, huh? You can use this to edit any text within the document. Figure 8.2 shows you what this looks like. (This is WDFT08-02.html on the companion Web site.)

Okay, that's about it for inline style. Let's learn about embedded CSS.

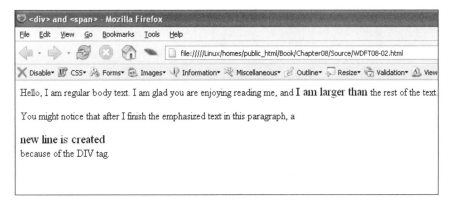

FIGURE 8.2 <DIV> vs. <SPAN>.

Embedded Style Sheets

Embedded style is a lot different than inline style. Unlike inline, embedded requires the use of a whole new tag: `<STYLE></STYLE>`. This tag includes all the information for the style of the entire page.

> **Tag—`<STYLE></STYLE>`**
> This is used to define the style sheets for the entire Web page in the `<HEAD>` section.

The `<STYLE></STYLE>` tag is defined in the header of the document. The header is within the `<HEAD></HEAD>` tag, before the body is initialized.

The format of the embedded style sheets is a lot different than inline style sheets as well. You don't have anyplace to add a `STYLE` attribute to a tag, and consequently, the style properties and values look a lot different. Here's what the code would look like using embedded style sheets:

```
<HTML>
<HEAD>
<TITLE> Embedded Style Sheets</TITLE>

<STYLE TYPE="text/css">
SPAN {color: gray}
P {text-align: center}
</STYLE>

</HEAD>

<BODY>

I am an Embedded Style Sheet.
<P> Notice that all paragraphs are automatically aligned to the center.</P>
And also notice that all text which uses <SPAN>the &lt SPAN &gt tag</SPAN> is
automatically gray!

</BODY>
</HTML>
```

What does this look like? Figure 8.3 shows you. (This is WDFT08-03.html on the companion Web site.)

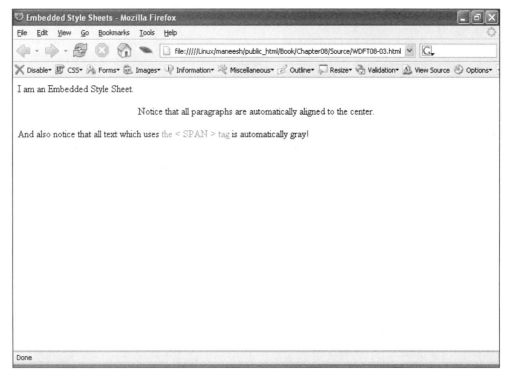

FIGURE 8.3 *Embedded style sheets.*

Let's examine the program. The main section of code is in the header of the page, before the body. Notice the `<STYLE></STYLE>` tags:

```
<STYLE TYPE="text/css">
SPAN {color: gray}
P {text-align: center}
</STYLE>
```

This is where all the magic happens. The first part is the `<STYLE>` tag, which tells the browser that the following will be part of a style sheet. Each tag's style is then adjusted by delineating the tag name (`SPAN`), followed by the property name and value within curly brackets (`{color: gray}`). If you want to adjust more than one property, add a semicolon after the property and value, and then add a new property. So if you wanted to adjust the font of the `<SPAN>` tag as well as the color, you could write something like this:

```
SPAN {color: gray; font: 12pt arial}
```

This makes everything inside <SPAN></SPAN> tags both gray and 12-point Arial.

You can add any tags that you want to adjust a style. It's a good idea to use the style sheet to set up the background. Adjust the <BODY> tag so that it looks like the following:

```
<STYLE TYPE="text/css">
BODY {background-image: url("background.gif")}
</STYLE>
```

This gives you more control over your background image, and you can also choose background colors and other properties to make your page look good.

Using embedded style sheets requires a bit of caution. Older browsers that don't support style sheets don't recognize the <STYLE></STYLE> tag, and they display any text that appears inside the tag. Take a look at what WDFT08-03.html looks like in an old version of Netscape (see Figure 8.4).

Look at that! The style sheets don't work, and the actual style sheet text is displayed! This can look pretty bad to the visitor.

Fortunately, you can fix this with a little extra code. Remember how to write comments using the <!-- and --> symbols? Well, if you surround the style sheet code with the comment symbols, the style sheet text won't appear onscreen, but the style will still work on browsers that support CSS. Note that if the browser doesn't support CSS, the style still won't work, but at least it won't display the style sheet code onscreen.

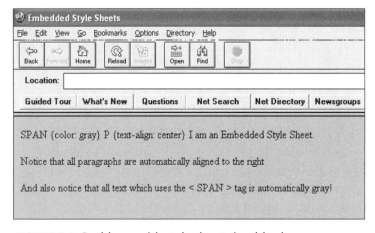

FIGURE 8.4 *Problems with style sheets in older browsers.*

Figure 8.5 shows the code from WDFT08-04.html after being rewritten for maximum compatibility.

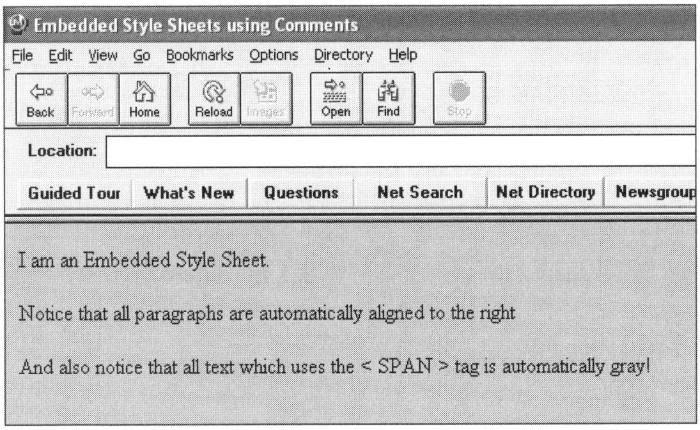

FIGURE 8.5 *Achieving compatibility with older browsers.*

What's the code that makes this work?

```
<STYLE TYPE="text/css">
<!--
SPAN {color: gray}
P {text-align: center}
-->
</STYLE>
```

Not too difficult, right?

That's it for embedded style sheets. Let's try out linked style sheets, the most powerful of the three types.

Linked Style Sheets

Linked style sheets are pretty similar to embedded style sheets, except that they don't appear between <STYLE></STYLE> tags. Instead, they're written in a totally different document and then linked to within the HTML page.

For example, take the style sheet from WDFT08-03.html. Let's say you want to make this an external linked style sheet. The first thing you should do is create a new file called style.css. (The name can be anything, as long the suffix is .css.)

In this case, the .css file will contain the following:

```
SPAN {color: gray}
P {text-align: center}
```

Figure 8.6 shows the file in Notepad.

Now you need to link the file to a Web page:

```
<HEAD>
<TITLE> External Style Sheets </TITLE>
```

```
<LINK REL="stylesheet" TYPE="text/css"
HREF="style.css" />
```

```
</HEAD>
```

FIGURE 8.6 *Style.css in Notepad.*

The format of `<LINK>` is a little different than that of most HTML tags. First of all, the `REL` attribute tells the browser that this file uses CSS. Next, the `TYPE` attribute tells the browser which type of file to use. Lastly, the `HREF` attribute gives the browser the location of the file.

Tag—`<LINK>`
This allows you to add externally linked style sheets to your page.

note

Note that the end of the `<LINK>` tag ends with `/>`. This defines the end of the tag. Although this isn't required for most tags, it's required for `<LINK>`.

Figure 8.7 shows how the entire page looks now. (This is WDFT08-05.html on the companion Web site.)

It looks exactly the same as WDFT08-04.html! That's because all of the styles are the same, but they've been copied from an external file rather than being embedded directly into the page.

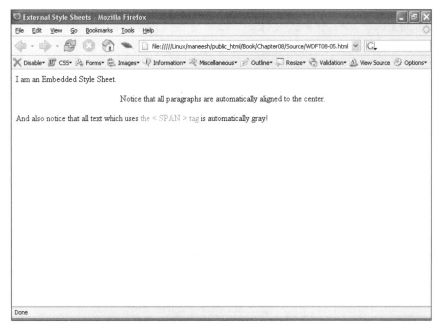

FIGURE 8.7 *Externally linked styles.*

WHY WOULD YOU EVER USE EXTERNAL STYLE SHEETS?

It might seem strange to use externally linked style sheets when you can embed the code directly into a page. However, you should stick with linked style sheets on most Web sites, because then all of the pages on your site can link to the single style sheet file.

Let's say you have 20 pages on your Web site, and you want to change the background of every page from one image to another. If you've used embedded style sheets (or even worse, the `<BODY></BODY>` tag), you need to open up each page and change it directly. This might not seem like *too* much work for 20 pages, but think about a site like Amazon.com. If they wanted to change one style factor on all their pages, they would need to open thousands of files manually!

Fortunately, style sheets include all the necessary information in one file. When you make a change to the style sheet itself, the change is reflected on all of your pages! Pretty cool, huh? Using linked style sheets will save you a lot of time.

Okay, now you understand the three types of Cascading Style Sheets. The only thing left is to learn about all of the properties you can adjust using style sheets.

Cascading Style Sheet Properties

There are a lot of style sheet properties. A *lot*. Fortunately, I put most of them in Appendix A, so you can find out which ones you need. I will give you a few of the most important ones now, though.

Table 8.1 lists the most important properties.

Table 8.1 Important CSS Properties

Property	Description	Value
font-family	Sets the font face (typeface) of the element	Font_String (Name of any font)
color	Sets the color of any text	RGB value of defined color
background-image	Sets the background image; only for use with the `<BODY>` tag	LocationOfImage
height	Sets the height of any element	Size
line-height	Sets the height between lines of text	Size
width	Sets the width of any element	Size

As you can see, this is a very short list. There are a lot more properties, but you probably won't be using them all. Check out the list in Appendix A.

Summary

That wraps up the chapter on CSS. There are some advanced CSS topics that we didn't go over, such as classes and IDs, but you can learn a lot more about them online. Go to the *Web Design for Teens* section of maneeshsethi.com and look for resources on how to do advanced CSS.

In this chapter, you learned the following:

❖ The definition of Cascading Style Sheets
❖ How to use inline style sheets
❖ How to use embedded style sheets
❖ How to use externally linked style sheets
❖ Some more CSS properties

That's it for Chapter 8, and also for Part 2! We're moving on to the basics of design in Part 3, so get ready.

PART 3

WEB
DESIGN

for
teens

Breaking into Design

In this part, we are going to begin discussing the art of design. The preceding chapters centered on the code to make Web pages, and this part will examine how to use that code to make navigable and interesting Web sites. We will be using Nvu a little more in this section to ease the work of actual coding.

Chapter 9
Navigation

Welcome back to the book! Are you ready for Part 3? This part will discuss design. It will go over tactics for making your pages look appealing and strategies for writing code to make the pages functional. Of course, knowing how to make a page look good is very important, so Part 3 focuses on the elements of design.

In this chapter, you'll learn about the basics of navigation. We'll go over the numerous forms of navigation and talk about their good and bad parts. Then you'll learn how to make a navigation bar with tables using Nvu.

Are you ready? Let's get started.

The Basics of Navigation

What is navigation? It's a way for your Web site visitors to move between pages.

The most important part about navigation is that it should almost never take more than two clicks to move from one page on your Web site to another. Depending on the situation,

Navigation

This is how you allow visitors to move between pages of your Web site. Without navigation, visitors can't visit any page except the home page.

it can sometimes be three clicks, but two clicks is generally the best method. If it takes more than two clicks to get from one section on your site to another, you should think about redesigning it so that moving between pages is easier.

Let's go over the different types of navigation.

The Navigation Bar

The first method is to use a navigation bar. This is simply a bar that contains numerous links to different sections of the Web site. Figure 9.1 shows the navigation bar for Amazon.com.

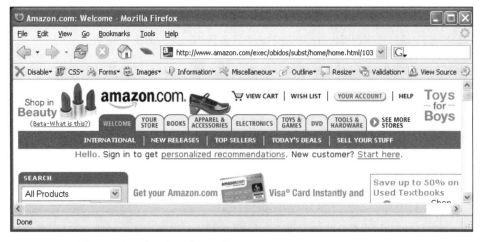

FIGURE 9.1 *The navigation bar from Amazon.com.*

Take a look at the main elements. There are numerous tabs that refer to different sections of the Web site: Welcome, Electronics, Tools & Hardware, and so forth. Within each section there are some subsections, such as Top Sellers and Today's Deals in the Welcome tab.

This type of horizontal navigation bar is found on many Web sites (www.maneeshsethi.com, for one).

Some Web sites use a vertical bar instead. Take a look at the old version of maneeshsethi.com in Figure 9.2.

A little different, right? Instead of being on the top of the page, the navigation bar is to the left.

Let's talk about the pros and cons of each style.

FIGURE 9.2 *A vertical navigation bar from the old maneeshsethi.com.*

Vertical Navigation Bars

Good:

❖ Because monitors are wider than they are tall, a vertical bar takes up a smaller percentage of the screen than a horizontal bar.

❖ These bars force the body of the document to be narrower, with fewer characters per line, making the document easier to read.

Bad:

❖ The bar goes down the entire side of the page, so the user keeps seeing it when he scrolls down.

❖ It can get in the way of the text and make it harder to read.

Horizontal Navigation Bars

Good:

❖ Horizontal bars are out of the way of the actual document, so the visitor can scroll past the bar and read the page.

❖ They can be easier to read because they're written horizontally, as the eyes of most people in the Western world are accustomed to reading.

Bad:

❖ If the bar gets too large, the visitor may have to scroll down to read the document, which can be very annoying.

❖ Unlike with vertical bars, the visitor may have to scroll up to the top of the page to move to another section of the site.

So there you have it, horizontal versus vertical. I suggest horizontal navigation bars, just because I find them easier to read and more out of the way. That's why I converted maneeshsethi.com from vertical to horizontal. Choose the method *you* like better, though.

Another thing I want you to notice: The links in the original version of maneeshsethi.com are text links, but in the new version they're images. Why would anyone do text links? Well, they give you a much better position on search engines such as Google. Because many search engines read the links on each site, text links are rated far higher than image links. Google puts a higher value on text links because many images are used for advertising, so text links make the search engine know that the link is informational and more useful. You can take advantage of this to drive traffic to your sites.

Now, you might be thinking that text links don't look as good as images, but you can make them look a lot better with style sheets. Take a look at my brother Ramit Sethi's page, http://www.ramitsethi.com, in Figure 9.3.

Those almost look like images, right? Well, they're actually text links, and they really help run up traffic on his site.

The reason they look stylish is because of the boxes behind them. These boxes help emphasize the words. When you're designing your Web site, you should experiment until you have the most attractive site possible.

Sometimes, however, you need to sacrifice pretty for functional. This means make sure your pages can be used by everyone first, before you make it look awesome. Sometimes you will have to substitute lower-quality pictures for higher ones because it speeds up the Web page, so make sure you test the site before you put it on the Web.

FIGURE 9.3 *Stylish text links in www.ramitsethi.com.*

High-Tech Navigation

There are some other types of navigation, but they're too rare or difficult to go into in-depth here. We'll just be taking a glancing look at them. (You can learn more about them on your own, though.)

The first type is a high-tech animated navigation scheme. Some sites use such high-tech schemes to conserve space. For example, Figure 9.4 shows the drop-down menus on www.udm4.com. These can be made with JavaScript.

It looks pretty cool, huh? The menu drops down when you put your mouse cursor over it, and when you move it away again, the menu disappears. This design allows the Web designer to pack lots of information into a small space.

Unfortunately, the benefits come at a cost. Because it's high-tech, some older browsers may not support it. If a visitor using an older browser can't use your navigation, he isn't going to visit your site again.

Also, high-tech navigation schemes are new and can be a little unusual and quirky. They might disturb some of your visitors. I don't really like them, because I would rather see all of my options at once than just a few at a time.

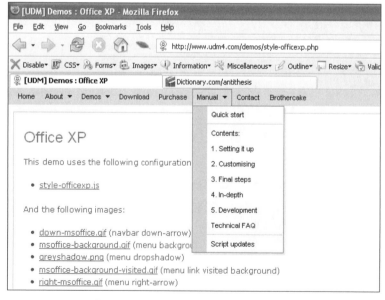

FIGURE 9.4 *High-tech menus on udm4.com.*

Site Maps

Another form of navigation is called a site map. This is a one-stop location that lists all of the pages on a Web site. For example, look at Figure 9.5, which shows part of Apple.com's site map.

Although this is only a portion of the entire site map, you can see its function. It lists out each category of the site, along with all related pages.

The nice thing about a site map is that it's a concentrated location that lists all the pages on the Web site. Unfortunately, the visitors must navigate through your pages in the first place to reach the site map.

For this reason, it's best to use site maps as a supplement to another navigation scheme. For example, Apple has a link on their main page that gives the user access to the site map (see Figure 9.6).

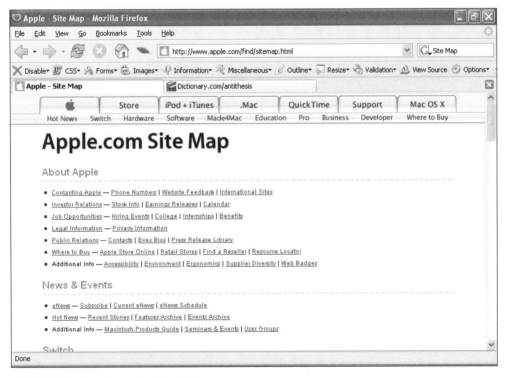

FIGURE 9.5 *Apple.com's site map.*

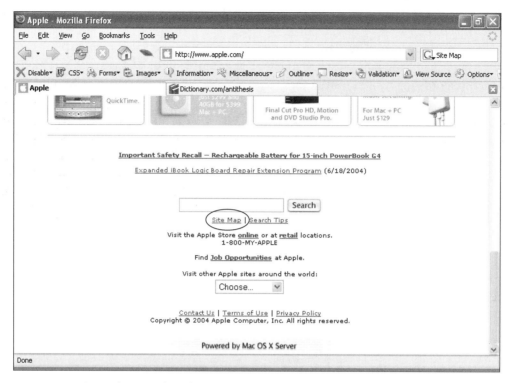

FIGURE 9.6 *Accessing Apple's site map.*

Site maps are very useful when you have a lot of different pages that can be easily separated into different categories.

Using Frames for Navigation

The last method of navigation uses frames, which allow a site to have two different pages loaded at the same time: one navigation bar and one main page. Take a look at Figure 9.7, which shows the frames on http://home.comcast.net/~chris.s/myth.html.

In this example, there are actually three frames. The first is the title bar that says *Myths & Legends*, the second is the navigation bar on the left, and the third is the content on the right.

Frames allow you to have a specific navigation bar that doesn't reload when the visitor goes to different pages on the Web site. However, frames can look a little bulky (the scroll bar in the navigation pane looks a little out of place), and they

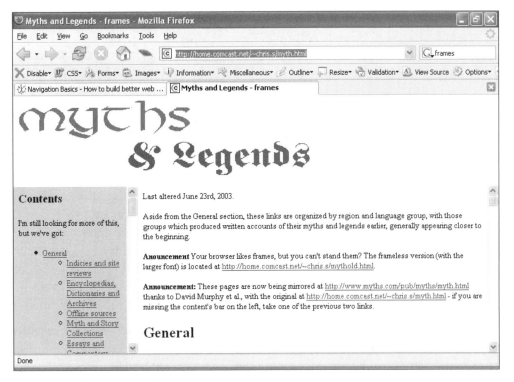

FIGURE 9.7 *Frames in action.*

make it very hard to bookmark or print the page. The printer prints the frames rather than the actual content, and the bookmark is only the top-level page. For these reasons, I recommend that you stay away from frames.

The next section will teach you how to create a navigation bar using Nvu. Make sure you have the program installed, and let's get ready to use it.

Building a Navigation Bar

Navigation bars are pretty difficult to build, but I'm going to walk you through the process. You're going to create a basic horizontal text navigation bar, and then you'll extend it by inserting images instead of text.

The first thing you need to do is come up with a basic site. Let's say it's a company site that has a homepage, a Catalog page where you sell some fake items, an About Us page, and a Contact Us page to let the visitor ask questions.

Let me walk you through the creation of a navigation bar, step by step. Although this one is definitely simple, you can expand it to make the bar look however you want.

First of all, open up Nvu. If you still haven't installed it, you can get it from the companion Web site or from www.nvu.com.

A blank window pops up. Within this window, you need to create a table. Select Table > Insert > Table (or click on the Table icon on the main toolbar), and a window like the one in Figure 9.8 pops up.

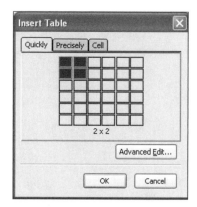

FIGURE 9.8 *The Insert Table dialog in Nvu.*

You've got quite a few options, eh? Well, for most navigation bars, you're only going to want one row, because you don't want the bar to take up too much vertical space. Set the number of columns to 1 as well, and make the border equal to 0.

You've just created the framework for the navigation bar! All you need to do is split up the table into a few individual cells so that you can add the buttons. To add a cell, just right-click on the table and select Table Insert > Column After. Do this three times.

Your table should look something like Figure 9.9.

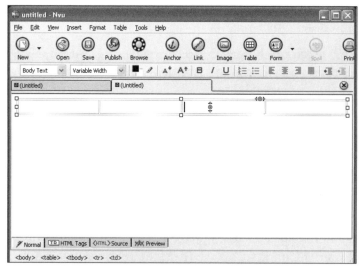

FIGURE 9.9 *Setting up the cells for a navigation bar.*

So what did you just do? You created a bar that has four cells, meaning you can add four different locations to the bar. For this example, call these four cells Home, Catalog, About Us, and Contact Us. Your window will look like Figure 9.10.

It's getting there, but the big problem now is that the items are too far apart. The page doesn't look good at all.

To fix this problem, you just need to add an extra blank cell to the beginning of the table. This moves the bar a little to the right. This does two things. One, it offsets the navigation bar from the left so that it doesn't appear to run off the screen, and two, it allows you to change the sizes of the other cells.

Let's add another cell. Right-click on the first cell in the table and select Table Insert > Column Before. An extra cell appears before the Home cell.

This new cell takes up half the table, making each cell pretty small. Don't worry about the size of it yet, though. You can adjust that later. First of all, let's make each of the title cells the proper length.

You want each cell to be just big enough to contain the text. To do this, highlight all of the cells that have words in them and right-click them. From the menu that opens, choose Table Cell Properties. The resulting window looks like Figure 9.11.

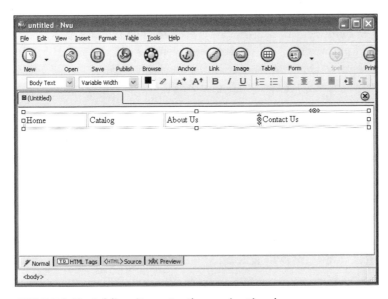

FIGURE 9.10 *Adding items to the navigation bar.*

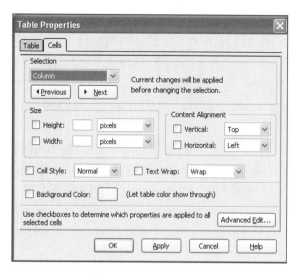

FIGURE 9.11 *The Table Properties window.*

So what do you do if you want to make each cell very small? You can set their width to only 1 pixel, so that each cell will expand to contain the text inside it but no larger.

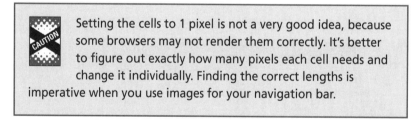

Setting the cells to 1 pixel is not a very good idea, because some browsers may not render them correctly. It's better to figure out exactly how many pixels each cell needs and change it individually. Finding the correct lengths is imperative when you use images for your navigation bar.

Now you can adjust the width of the indentation cell on the left. Right-click on the cell and change its width to whatever you want the indentation to be. For this project, choose 10 percent. Click on the units box next to the Width text box to change the unit of measurement from pixels to percent. The result will look like Figure 9.12.

Uh-oh! All of the items are spaced too far apart again! To fix this, you need to add another blank cell to the end of the table. (Don't change the right indentation width, or else the items will still be spaced too far apart.) Your table now looks like Figure 9.13!

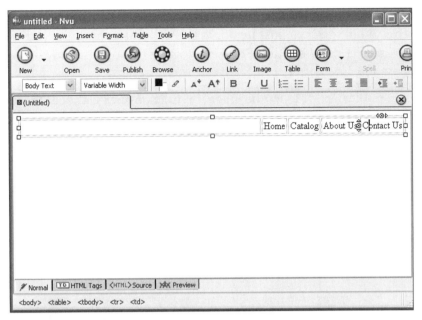

FIGURE 9.12 *Adjusting the indentation tab on the navigation bar.*

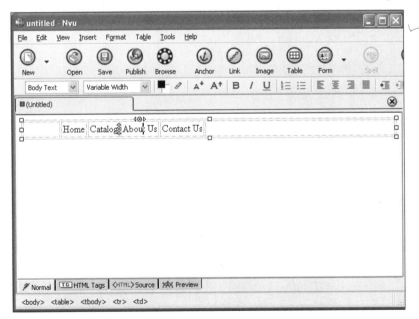

FIGURE 9.13 *Adding a right indent to the navigation bar.*

Okay, so you've designed the bar. It doesn't do anything unless you add links, though. To add links in Nvu, just highlight the text you want to link, right-click, and select Create Link. The Link Properties dialog box opens, and you can add your local or absolute link there.

For this example, set the Home page to index.html, Catalog to catalog/catalog.html, About Us to about/about.html, and Contact Us to contact/contact.html. This means that all of these items need to be in subdirectories of the folder that contains index.html. Figure 9.14 shows the file structure.

Now that you've got this set up, Figure 9.15 shows what the page actually looks like!

Sure, it doesn't look that great, but it isn't bad either. Notice that the bar is above the main section of the screen, so it doesn't take up a lot of space.

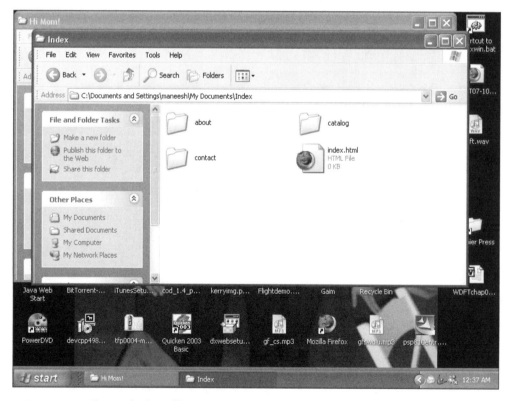

FIGURE 9.14 *The Web site's file structure.*

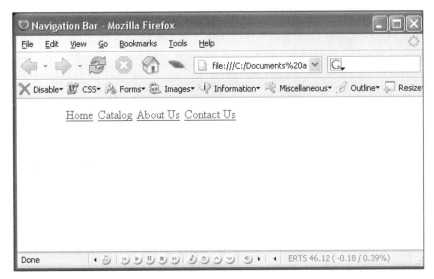

FIGURE 9.15 *The final text navigation bar.*

Of course, if you want to spice things up a little, you can add some images. I made a collection of images in Macromedia Fireworks. It's a pretty expensive imaging program (~$300), but it does the job well and there's a trial edition on the companion Web site. Let's add some of these images to the navigation bar.

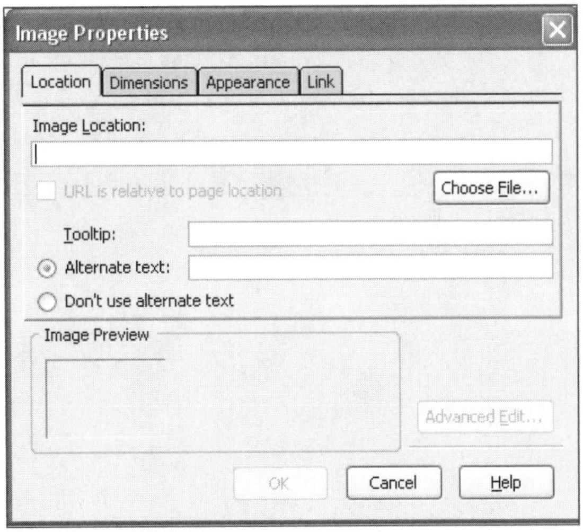

First of all, highlight the text and delete it. Then click in the home tag and click the Image button on the main toolbar. This brings up the Image Properties dialog, pictured in Figure 9.16.

FIGURE 9.16 *The Image Properties dialog box.*

From here, you can link to the images in the images directory in the Chapter 9 folder on the companion Web site. First of all, browse for a file you want to use in the Image Location field, and then add alternate text. Alternate text is extra information about the image that appears when the viewer moves his mouse over it. In addition, this can help a blind person who visits the site, if he has software that can read the alternate tags to him out loud. Search engines like Google also place value on alternate text, helping get your Web site better results on their search.

After adding the alternate text and creating the link, go to the Link tab in the Image Properties dialog box and add a link to that page. Do this for all of the links, and your navigation bar will look something like Figure 9.17.

Looking a little better, eh? However, that white space between each image is a little ugly, so let's get rid of it.

Remember cell padding and cell spacing? Well, here's where it really makes a difference. The cell padding and spacing create some white space around each of the cells, which helps make the text look a little better on the screen. However, this extra space doesn't look so great with this particular navigation bar, so let's get rid of it.

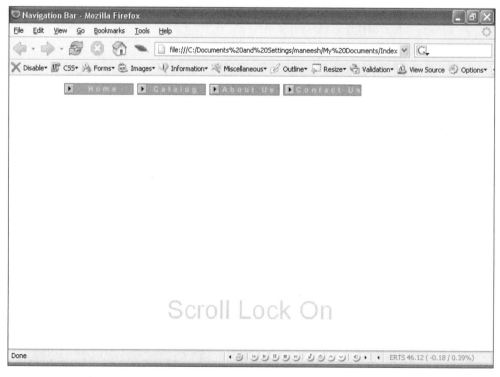

FIGURE 9.17 *The navigation bar.*

First, of all, select the table by right-clicking on it and choosing Table Select > Table from the menu that pops up. All of the cells in the window should be highlighted. Right-click on the table and choose Table Properties. The Table Properties window pops open, as shown in Figure 9.18.

See those options for cell spacing and cell padding? Change them both to 0. Then click OK and watch the results. The final version of the page should look like Figure 9.19.

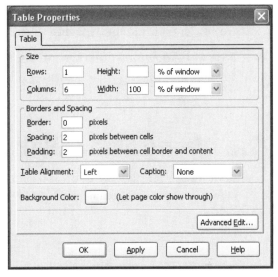

FIGURE 9.18 *The Table Properties dialog box.*

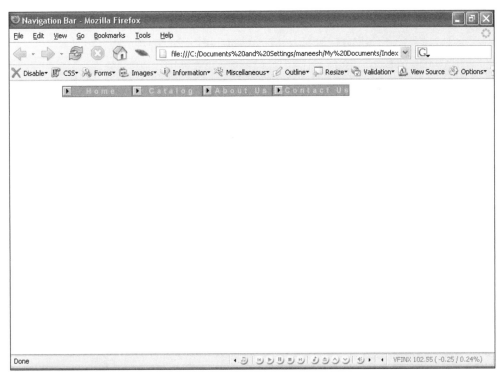

FIGURE 9.19 *The completed image navigation bar page in index.html.*

Looks a lot better, huh? These images were designed to be attached, and getting rid of the padding and spacing does the trick.

Now you know how to create an entire navigation bar! You just need something for it to link to, and that's covered in the next few chapters. Before we move on, though, let's take a look at the source code for the page we created.

The Navigation Bar HTML Source

Nvu doesn't do a very good job of keeping the HTML source easy to understand. Nonetheless, it still isn't too hard to interpret:

```
<html>
<head>
<meta content="text/html; charset=ISO-8859-1"
http-equiv="content-type">
<title>Navigation Bar</title>
</head>
<body>
<table style="width: 100%; text-align: left;" border="0" cellpadding="0"
cellspacing="0">
<tbody>
<tr>
<td style="width: 10%; vertical-align: top;"><br>
</td>
<td style="vertical-align: top; width: 1px;"><a href="index.html"><img
alt="Visit the Index" title="Visit the Index" src="images/home.gif"
style="border: 0px solid ; width: 115px; height: 18px;"></a> <br>
</td>
<td style="vertical-align: top; width: 1px;"><a
href="catalog/catalog.html"><img alt="Catalog" title="Catalog"
src="images/catalog.gif"
style="border: 0px solid ; width: 115px; height: 18px;"></a><br>
</td>
```

```
<td style="white-space: nowrap; vertical-align: top; width: 1px;"><a
href="about/about.html"><img alt="About Us" title="About Us"
src="images/about.gif"
style="border: 0px solid ; width: 115px; height: 18px;"></a><br>
</td>
<td style="white-space: nowrap; vertical-align: top; width: 1px;"><a
href="contact/contact.html"><img alt="Contact Us"
title="Contact Us" src="images/contact.gif"
style="border: 0px solid ; width: 127px; height: 18px;"></a><br>
</td>
<td style="vertical-align: top; width: 75%">
</td>
</tr>
</tbody>
</table>
</body>
</html>
```

You'll notice a lot of style sheets in here. Nvu uses style sheets to make a lot of their items work, but everything can be done in HTML just as easily.

Take a look at the `<table></table>` section. Notice how it refers to the padding and shading of the cells. Your selection in the menu is reflected here in the source code.

There isn't much to say about the source. Just look over it and make sure you understand everything about it, because it will help you if you want to edit that toolbar.

Summary

Whew! You've survived the first chapter of Part 3. We're putting together everything you've learned and applying it to building a Web site, so it's a little different than the HTML chapters.

In this chapter, you learned the following:

❖ The different navigation types

❖ How to build a navigation bar

❖ How to read the source of a navigation bar

In the next chapter, you're going to learn how to arrange your pages to make them look good. I hope you're ready!

Chapter 10
Choosing and Creating Images

In this chapter, you're going to learn about images. First we'll look at the types of images you'll want to include on a page. Even if an image looks really cool, you need to take a few things into consideration before you use it on your Web page, such as its color and file size.

Then you'll learn how to procure and use images. There are a lot of Web sites with free images for anyone to use and many sites that offer images for sale. A lot of times, if you see an image you really like on someone's personal site, they'll let you use it if you e-mail them and ask. However, it is illegal to steal images off someone's site, so make sure you get permission first.

Then you'll learn how to make images of your own. You'll use Macromedia Fireworks to create some basic images, and you can adjust these images to fit your Web page perfectly.

Choosing Images

Choosing the images you want to use can be a tough job. There are so many images out there, and many of them look so cool. However, you can use only a select few, and they need to be perfectly designed to fit your Web page.

Images play a big role in the presentation of your Web site. For example, take a look at Figure 10.1.

What do you see? I see a page that has some pretty bad design. Let's talk about what they did wrong.

First of all, notice that the background image isn't stretched to fit my browser. The image is tiled, meaning that you see multiple copies of it laid across the screen. It doesn't look very good.

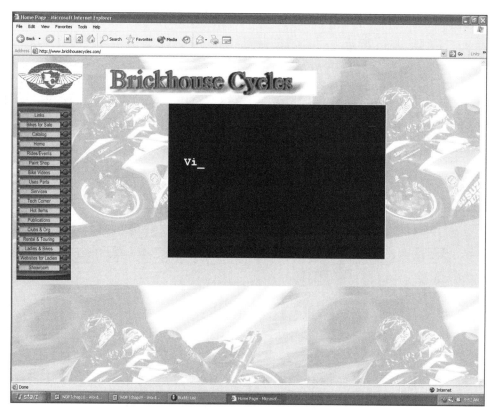

FIGURE 10.1 *Bad design on brickhousecycles.com.*

Now, granted, I'm using a bigger resolution for this image than most monitors do. I use 1280x1024, and most monitors still use 800x600 or 1024x768. But still, there are a lot of people who use big resolutions. This background image truly alienates anyone who visits the site, because it makes the page very unappealing.

Also, notice the title bar, the one that says Brickhouse Cycles, and the logo to the left. The background of the images is white, but the background of the page isn't. This creates a big conflict and makes the title stand out, in a bad way.

As you can see, these images make a big difference in the quality of the page. There are a few things you can do to fix the problems.

First of all, don't use this background image. The color is red and blue, and it conflicts with the actual page. You don't want your visitors spending more time looking at the background than what's on top of it.

Second, make the background of the images transparent so they'll work with a background of any color. As you can see in the image, the text "Brickhouse Cycles" has a white background upon a different background image. If the background of the text is transparent, then the white color wouldn't appear, and the text would appear to be right on top of the background. Transparency is easy to do, and it really makes a page look better.

There are some other things that this page could do better, so take a look at it and make a list of things you could improve. Doing lists like this will sharpen your design skills.

Now that you know about some of the problems that can come from using images badly, let's talk about what you should do to make them look good.

Choosing the Right Images

Picking images is a little difficult. First of all, you need to know which types of images fit best with your page design. For example, you don't want your image to look anything like the one in Figure 10.2.

FIGURE 10.2 *Ugly image design in badfireworksimage.jpg.*

This image probably doesn't look that bad in grayscale, but open up badfireworksimage.jpg on the companion Web site and you'll notice that the background is bright green. This color detracts from the fireworks image.

Maxim #8

"Your images should always stand out. Not just against the background, but against the text also."

Because of this, your images should stand out against everything else on the page. Images establish a presence, and without them, your page will look boring and unusable. It's bad enough for the text to appear stronger than the images, but having the background conflict with them is a million times worse.

There's a saying in design that involves colors: "The first color is white. The second color is black. The third color is red." This saying refers to the best colors that you can use in design. The greatest possible emphasis is black text on a white background. When you want to vary your color, red is the next best choice because it's a primary color that's in direct contrast to black and white.

That's why Web sites with lime-green text on a black background are incredibly difficult to read. The same thing happens with images. When you have an image with a background, it will look good in contrast with white or red. The emphasis makes your images look better to your visitors.

Take a look at Figure 10.3, which shows redhat.com. This is printed in grayscale, of course, but check out the redhat.jpg file on the companion Web site to see the good use of color.

Red Hat uses very good contrast in their images, with the black, white, and red standing out. Although they include a few shades of brown and gray as well, you can see how the red stands out against everything else on the page. This makes reading and understanding the images a lot easier. As you can see, the contrast makes the page pleasing to the eye.

Now that you know the basics of color, let's apply this knowledge to images. Your photographs won't conform directly to a color scheme, of course, but any images that involve text or basic shapes can be melded into your page's style.

The next section will teach you how to use your own images on your Web page.

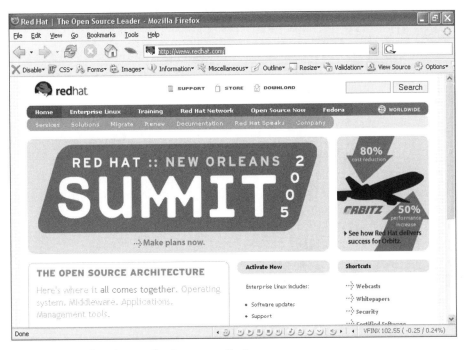

FIGURE 10.3 *Good use of color on redhat.com.*

Putting Images on a Web Page

Using your own images on your Web page isn't too difficult. You need to use the `<IMG>` tag, which you learned about in Chapter 5, "Working with Images and Text." You just need to find a photo you want to use, put it in the same directory as a subdirectory of the main page, and use the `<IMG>` tag to link to it. Let's try it with the same page that you used to make a navigation bar in the previous chapter.

Figure 10.4 is a picture of a road. You're going to insert this into your page as a logo.

Remember the navigation bar you had earlier? Let's add the logo to the left of it, to make it look good.

FIGURE 10.4 *The logo for your page.*

FIGURE 10.5 *Inserting the image.*

Uh-oh, there's a problem. Two problems, actually. First of all, the image is way too large. Secondly, the image is above the navigation bar, even though they would look better side-by-side.

Let's take things one step at a time. Take a look at the code and see if you can identify the problem with the location of the image on the screen:

```
<body>
<img alt="Fake Logo" src="images/logo.jpg">
<table style="width: 100%; text-align: left;" border="0" cellpadding="0"
 cellspacing="0">
  <tbody>
    <tr>
      <td style="width: 10%; vertical-align: top;"><br>
      </td>
      <td style="vertical-align: top; width: 1px;"><a href="index.html"><img
alt="Visit the Index" title="Visit the Index" src="images/home.gif"
style="border: 0px solid ; width: 115px; height: 18px;"></a> <br>
```

```
    </td>
    <td style="vertical-align: top; width: 1px;"><a
href="catalog/catalog.html"><img alt="Catalog" title="Catalog"
src="images/catalog.gif"
style="border: 0px solid ; width: 115px; height: 18px;"></a><br>
    </td>
    <td style="white-space: nowrap; vertical-align: top; width: 1px;"><a
href="about/about.html"><img alt="About Us" title="About Us"
src="images/about.gif"
style="border: 0px solid ; width: 115px; height: 18px;"></a><br>
    </td>
    <td style="white-space: nowrap; vertical-align: top; width: 1px;"><a
href="contact/contact.html"><img alt="Contact Uscontact/"
title="Contact Us" src="images/contact.gif"
style="border: 0px solid ; width: 127px; height: 18px;"></a><br>
    </td>
    <td style="vertical-align: top;">
    </td>
  </tr>
 </tbody>
</table>
</body>
```

So what's wrong with this? The code for the image is outside of the table. This effectively pushes the table down so that your image can be on top.

 note Notice that the tags in this code aren't capitalized, and that they use style sheets very prevalently. This is because the code was generated by Nvu in the last chapter. It would be a good idea to capitalize all of these HTML tags once you get the final version of the Web page.

The code should look like this instead:

```
<body>
<table style="width: 100%; text-align: left;" border="0" cellpadding="0"
 cellspacing="0">
  <tbody>
    <tr>
      <td style="width: 10%; vertical-align: top;">
<img alt="Fake Logo" src="images/logo.jpg";">
<br>
      </td>
```

```
    <td style="vertical-align: top; width: 1px;"><a href="index.html"><img
alt="Visit the Index" title="Visit the Index" src="images/home.gif"
style="border: 0px solid ; width: 115px; height: 18px;"></a> <br>
    </td>
<!-- Rest of Table -->
</tr>
</table>
</body>
```

Looks a little better, huh? The resulting Web page looks something like Figure 10.6.

Sure, at least the page is aligned a little better, but that image is still way too big! You need to shrink it down.

There are two ways to reduce an image's size: the good way and the bad way. I'm going to teach you the bad way now, and later on we'll go over the good way.

FIGURE 10.6 *The fixed location of the image.*

The bad way involves using the WIDTH and HEIGHT attributes to make the browser redefine the height of the image. You add these two attributes into the <IMG> tag, and the browser draws the image at the specified size on the screen. If you use this method, keep in mind that the measurement should be in pixels, which is different on each monitor depending on its resolution. Figure 10.7 shows the page with the scaled-down image.

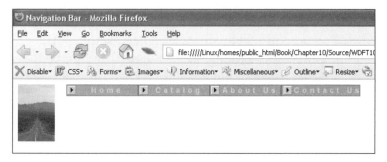

FIGURE 10.7 *The fixed size of the image.*

> You don't actually *need* to use pixels. With style sheets, you can use inches if you like. Just remove the WIDTH and HEIGHT attributes from your code and add some style sheets. You might write <IMG SRC=image.jpg STYLE="width: 2.5in; height: 3in"> or something like that. Just adding the in after the value converts the measurement into inches rather than pixels.

Let's take a quick look at the image code.

```
<td style="width: 10%; vertical-align: top;"><img alt="Fake Logo"
src="images/logo.jpg" HEIGHT=89 WIDTH=60>
```

It's looking a little better, but you can make it nicer still. We'll go over how in the next section.

So why is this the bad way to change the size of images? Unfortunately, the browser must still load the big version of the image (the one that was 270x400 pixels), and then it resizes the image and displays the smaller one (89x60 pixels). This means that it will take a lot longer to load the site than it should. In addition, the image won't be as crisp as if you resize it manually.

You'll learn how to adjust file size in the next section.

Image Editing

In this section, you're going to learn how to create and edit images. This is by no means a full primer on how to use an image-editing program, nor will it teach you how to do everything you want with images. This is just a brief overview.

For this chapter, you're going to use Macromedia Fireworks, which you can download from my Web site, www.maneeshsethi.com. This is a great program, but it's only one of the two imaging programs that come with this book. The other one is JASC Paint Shop Pro (also available on www.maneeshsethi.com), one of my favorite image-editing programs. Although it isn't specialized for Web development like Fireworks is, it's still very useful if you want to make some nice images.

The first thing you need to do is install and open up Fireworks. Figure 10.8 shows what the program's interface looks like.

Click on Open in the main window, and a new window pops up that looks like Figure 10.9.

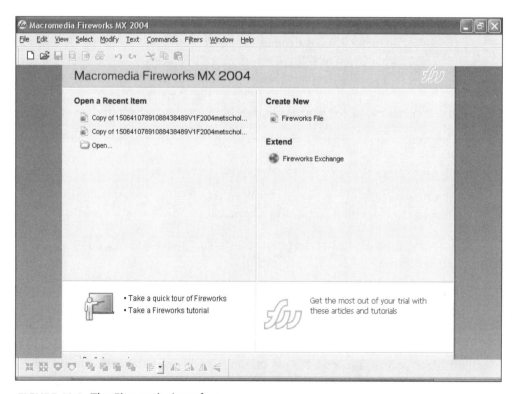

FIGURE 10.8 *The Fireworks interface.*

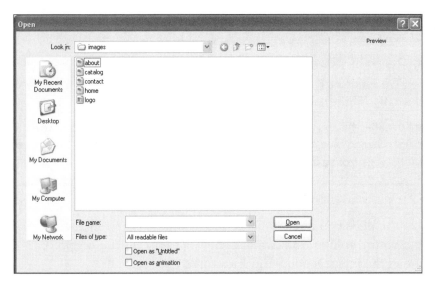

FIGURE 10.9 *The Open window.*

In the Chapter10 directory on the companion Web site, move into the images folder, and choose logo.jpg. Double-click the file to load it.

Now let's plan out which images to use and how they'll look. Let's take that fake company's site from the last chapter and expand on it.

The first thing to do is draw out the plan. Figure 10.10 shows a rough sketch I made of what the Web page will look like.

You're going to follow the rule of colors: black, white, and red. So, your text will be black, your background will be white, and your headers will be red.

FIGURE 10.10 *A rough draft of a Web page.*

> ### WHAT'S WITH THE SKETCH?
>
> Making a sketch of your Web page is one of the most important things you can do when you're designing it. Having an outline, no matter how rough it is, will really help the design of the page.
>
> Notice how ugly this rough draft is. I didn't even use a straight-edge. However, even this rough drawing gives you an idea how the page is going to look. It's a lot easier to model a page from a drawing than to pull it out of your head.

Let's take the page you already have, which was pictured in Figure 10.7. The first thing you're going to do is make the road look a little bit prettier. Figure 10.11 shows the image loaded into Fireworks.

Do you remember how the image looked on the actual Web page? Look back at Figure 10.6 if you don't. The road looks a little lopsided because the image is so big!

FIGURE 10.11 *The road image within Fireworks.*

There are a few ways to remedy this situation. You could simply scale down the image, as you did earlier. Scaling down an image decreases its file size and also allows for more elements on the actual page.

To scale down an image, first load it into Fireworks. Remember the dimensions you used for the scaled image earlier this chapter? It was 89x60 pixels. Let's resize the big image to 89x60 in Fireworks.

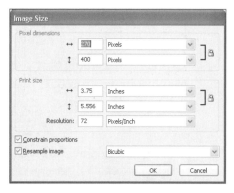

Once you've opened the file, go to Modify > Canvas Size > Image Size. A window like the one in Figure 10.12 pops up.

Now all you need to do is type in your numbers. Notice that when you change the width, the height automatically

FIGURE 10.12 *The Image Size window.*

changes. This is because Fireworks is maintaining the image's proportions. You want to go outside these proportions, however, so deselect the Constrain Proportions option. Then change the width to 60 pixels and the height to 80 pixels.

You now have a fully resized image. Pretty cool, huh? Let's make it even look better by getting rid of the lopsided effect. You can do this by turning the image into a circle and focusing on the major part of the image.

---

 note It's a lot easier to work with bigger images, so you'll be editing the large unscaled image and then resizing it later. In most cases, you'll want to do this.

The first thing you need to do is crop the image to a proper size. Cropping means removing a portion of an image, so that you can focus on the most important section.

 **Definition**

Cropping

This is a way to get rid of all the unnecessary information in an image. By using cropping, you keep the important part of the image and cut out the rest.

You need to cut off a large part of the sky. Figure 10.13 shows the new logo.

The top darker section will be cropped off, and the rest will remain. The final image looks like Figure 10.14.

So how do you crop images? In Fireworks, you need to select the Crop tool on the main toolbar (see Figure 10.15).

Highlight everything that you want to keep in the cropped image, and then double-click in the crop box. Everything that you've highlighted remains, and everything else disappears.

 Make sure you back up the image before cropping, because cropping actually removes data from the image. After you crop an image and close Fireworks, you won't be able to get the rest of the image back.

FIGURE 10.13 *The about-to-be-cropped logo.*

FIGURE 10.14 *The cropped logo.*

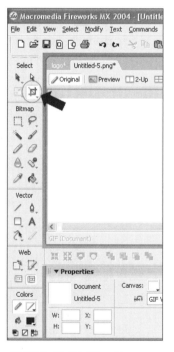

FIGURE 10.15 *The Crop tool.*

Let's see how this image looks within the Web page. Figure 10.16 shows the results of adding the rectangular image to the page. (This is WDFT10-04.html on the companion Web site.)

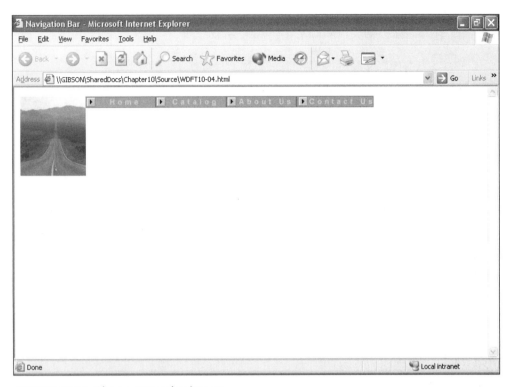

FIGURE 10.16 *The rectangular image.*

Now that you've cropped the image, let's make it look even cooler by turning it into a circle. To do this, you need to highlight the circle you want to crop out. Go to the Marquee tool, hold down the left mouse button, and select Oval Marquee. Figure 10.17 shows how it's done.

Now highlight the portion of the image that you want to keep. For this Web site, you want to highlight the center of the road, so draw a circle around that. After highlighting it, choose Select > Inverse. This selects everything except the circle that you just drew. Now press the Delete key and the background goes away, leaving just the circle in the foreground. This is shown in Figure 10.18.

Now all that's left to do is save the image. Because there's a blank background, you need to save the image as a GIF file. GIF files are the only type of images that allow

FIGURE 10.17 *The Oval Marquee tool.*

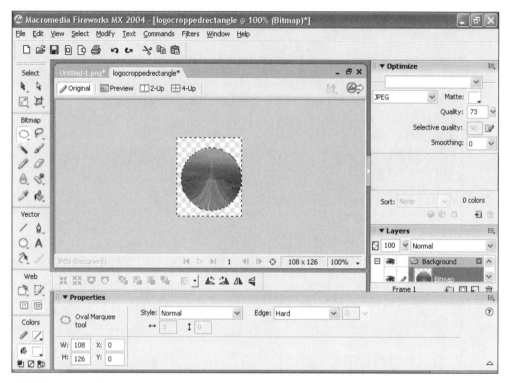

FIGURE 10.18 *The final circular selection.*

transparency, and you have transparency in this image as all of the background behind the circular foreground. You can tell that it is transparent because of the checkered background. Note that having a white background does not mean transparency—only a checkered background does.

Remember, GIF is not a good format for photos. It only works well with images with a few colors, so use JPEG for photos or images with lots of colors.

Saving requires a little bit of effort in Fireworks. First of all, you need to go to the File > Export Wizard option. A window may pop up recommending GIF or JPEG—just click OK and move on to the next section.

The next window shows the image and gives you a large number of options about how to change it. Most likely, the only thing you need to change is the file type from JPEG to GIF. After this, set the transparency option at the bottom of the window to Alpha transparency. Your final export window should look pretty close to Figure 10.19. Then click OK and save the file.

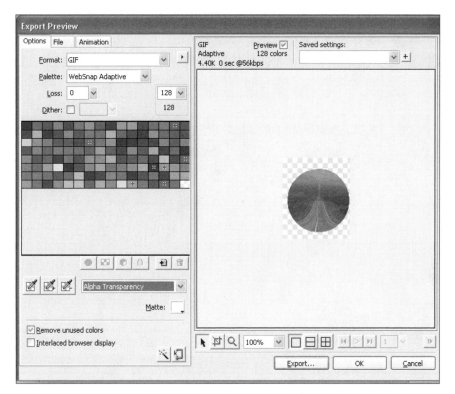

FIGURE 10.19 *The exporting window.*

Let's take one last look at how this circular image looks in a browser, as shown in Figure 10.20. (This is WDFT10-05.html on the companion Web site.)

For this screenshot I made a few specific changes, such as adding a cell between the image and the navigation bar to give it a little more depth, and centering all of the images in their cells. It looks pretty good.

You can check out the source in WDFT10-05.html. The major differences are that I added a new tab, and all of the `vertical-align` styles are now equal to `center`.

That's it for designing your own page. You'll use this page in the next chapter, which shows you how to work with text and fonts in your Web pages. In addition, we'll go over more tools of the imaging trade.

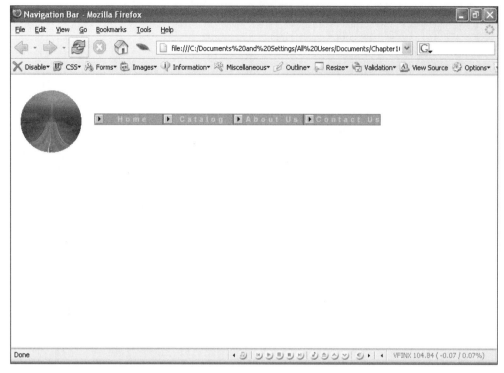

FIGURE 10.20 *The final circular selection.*

Summary

This was definitely a tough chapter! We went over a lot of the tricks of using images in your Web pages.

In this chapter, you learned the following:

❖ How to select the right images

❖ How to add the images to your page

❖ How to edit the images

That's all for Chapter 10. In the next chapter, you're going to learn more about text and fonts. Get ready!

Chapter 11

Working with Text

This chapter revolves around using text on a Web page. It will go over the best colors and fonts to use, and how you can use style sheets to make text even better. You'll also learn about spacing and margin tips in the page.

This chapter will also discuss images that display text. For example, a lot of Web pages have title bars at the top. Take a look at Figure 11.1, which is the title bar for maneeshsethi.com.

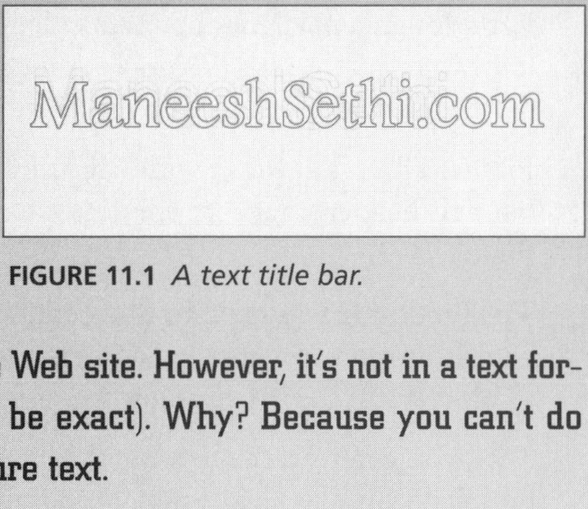

FIGURE 11.1 *A text title bar.*

This title bar is simply the URL of the Web site. However, it's not in a text format, but in an image format (GIF, to be exact). Why? Because you can't do those cool background effects with pure text.

Let's look at an even more obvious example of images that display text. Go to google.com and check out the title bar. Looks pretty cool, huh? That's because it uses numerous colors and drop shadows. These effects cannot be done with basic HTML, but they can be done within an imaging program.

You'll learn the methods to create these title bars later in the chapter, but first we need to talk about text in general.

Text Colors and Fonts

Remember when you learned about the "best colors" in Chapter 10? Take a look at Maxim #9 to refresh your memory.

These are the best colors to use in your designs because they complement each other. This doesn't mean you have to *limit* yourself to these three colors, of course, but they provide the best contrast with one another. Feel free to experiment until you create the design that best represents your site.

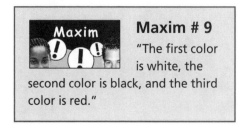

Maxim # 9
"The first color is white, the second color is black, and the third color is red."

For example, maneeshsethi.com has a white background, black text, and red headers. The contrast of this color scheme really helps to emphasize the text and the different sections.

Making text a certain color is easy with the `<FONT></FONT>` tag. You just need to add the `COLOR` attribute.

Let's design a page that involves colors and fonts. Using the same site from the last two chapters, let's design an About Us page. The About Us section is set up on the navigation bar already, so all you need to do is create the page.

First of all, let's start off with what you already have. You created the navigation bar and header image in previous chapters, so right now your page looks like Figure 11.2.

The first thing you need to do is add some text to the page. Unfortunately, the page isn't quite set up correctly, so adding text makes it look like Figure 11.3. (This is WDFT11-01.html on the companion Web site.)

Sure, you can read the text and it's in a decent font. However, the text is pretty boring because of its location. Sticking text at the far-left side of the screen isn't always the best way to go. For example, take a look at the book you are holding in your hands right now. You don't want the text to run off the page, into the crack in the middle, do you? Margins allow some breathing room for the text so that it is easier to read.

This Web page has a logo image in the top-left corner. In Figure 11.3, the text is directly aligned with the logo on the left border of the page. This makes the

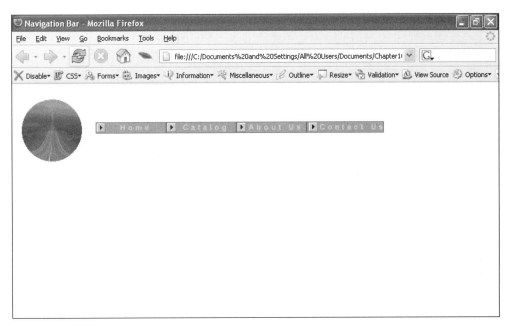

FIGURE 11.2 *The preliminary About Us page.*

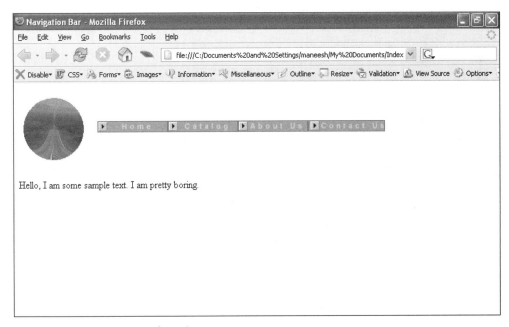

FIGURE 11.3 *Boring text location.*

page seem common and ordinary. A strictly ordinary design may be okay for research papers or essays, but you want your personal Web site to catch the reader's attention. You want it to be extraordinary!

There are a few tactics for catching the visitor's attention. Of course, you can always use bright flashing colors and animated images, but that's a really good way to annoy the visitor. The best way to make your page interesting is to break up your text in a simple, eye-pleasing way. Take a look at Figure 11.4, which shows Adobe.com.

What makes this page interesting to look at? There are a couple of really cool things that the designers did. First of all, they made the text start a few inches in from the right. This space, the *margin*, prevents the text from bleeding off the page.

The page also uses a photo, which catches your eye immediately. Notice how the photo goes into part of the text. This is called *text wrapping*, and it can be done in HTML. Text wrapping allows a picture to become part of the actual page and helps demonstrate the image's significance.

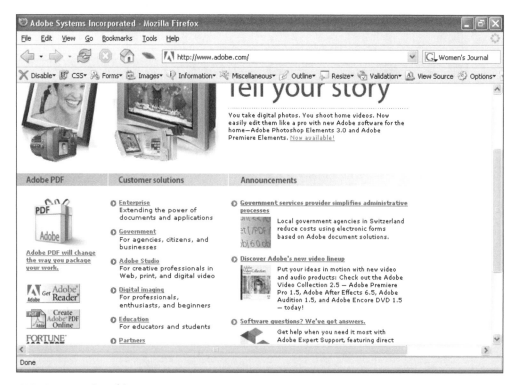

FIGURE 11.4 *Breaking up a page.*

To emphasize the text on this Web page, you're going to add margins to the side. These margins will help draw the reader's attention away from the logo and toward the main section of the page, the actual text.

Creating a margin for text is as easy as creating a blank table. Just open up the page in Nvu, move to a new line, and click Create New Table. Give it one row and two columns. Your table should look something like Figure 11.5.

Now, all you have to do is make the left column just as wide as you want it to be. This creates a margin that you can adjust to be as wide or as narrow as you want.

For this example, I made the left column 50 pixels wide. To do this, right-click in the left column, choose Table Cell Properties, and change the width of the table.

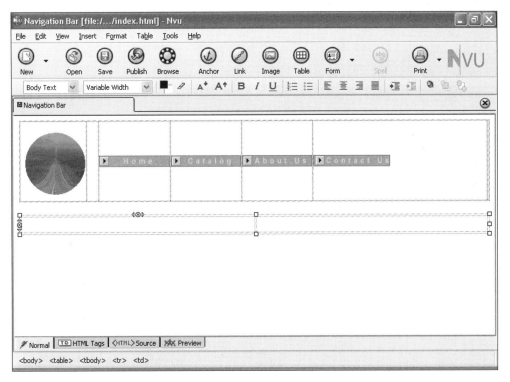

FIGURE 11.5 *Creating a table.*

Let's take a look at how to make this table in HTML. You just need to add the WIDTH property to the table tags:

```
<TABLE>
<TR>
<TD WIDTH=50></TD>
<TD>Hello, I am some sample text. I am not so boring anymore.
</TD>
</TR>
</TABLE>
```

This code sample creates a table with one row, adds two cells to that row, and makes the first one blank and 50 pixels wide. This indents the text.

When Nvu creates the table, it looks a little different. The following shows Nvu's default code:

```
<table style="width: 100%; text-align: left;" border="0" cellpadding="2"
cellspacing="2">
<tbody>
<tr>
<td style="width: 50px; vertical-align: top;"><br>
</td>
<td style="vertical-align: top;">Hello, I am some sample text. I
am not so boring anymore.<br>
</td>
</tr>
</tbody>
</table>
```

This is in WDFT11-02.html on the companion Web site.

Notice the subtle differences between the HTML version and Nvu's version. Nvu uses style sheets very extensively (a little *too* extensively, in my opinion). In addition, it adds some unnecessary information, such as the vertical-align style in the blank cell. This needless information obscures the meaning of your source code, so be careful when using Nvu.

Now that you know how to move text to the right, you should probably figure out what sort of text you want to add to the page in the first place. Because this is an About Us page, you want to provide some information relating to the company. It would be good to have a section that talks about the company and a section that gives the address and phone number.

Let's call the company Fake Company. You can add a header in Nvu using regular text. First you add text in regular fonts, and then you adjust the header sections to make it look better.

Let's add the text to the page first. Here it is:

About Fake Company

Fake Company was formed in 2004, the brainchild of John Fake. He truly enjoyed allowing people to experience Fake stuff, so he created this company to provide Fake goods to the public.

Fake's Beliefs:

❖ There should be Fake for everyone.
❖ Everything Fake is beautiful.
❖ There should be a worldwide understanding of Fake.

You can do this in Nvu. The code for the text section (table and all) looks like this:

```
<table style="width: 100%; text-align: left;" border="0" cellpadding="2"
 cellspacing="2">
  <tbody>
    <tr>
      <td style="width: 50px; vertical-align: top;"><br>
      </td>
      <td style="vertical-align: top;">About
Fake Company<br>
      <br>
Fake Company was formed in 2004, the brainchild of John
Fake. He truly enjoyed allowing people to experience Fake stuff, so he
created this company to provide Fake goods to the public.<br>
      <br>
Fake's Beliefs:<br>
      <ul>
        <li>There should be Fake for everyone.</li>
        <li>Everything Fake is beautiful.</li>
        <li>There should be a worldwide understanding of Fake.</li>
      </ul>
      </td>
    </tr>
  </tbody>
</table>
```

Figure 11.6 shows what this looks like. (This is WDFT11-03.html on the companion Web site.)

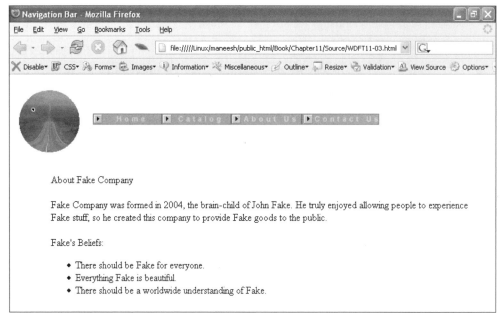

FIGURE 11.6 *Adding text.*

Now you can add formatting to the text. This is very simple in Nvu. Let's make the text red, Arial font, 14 points. Open up the file in Nvu and check out the text.

Obviously, the main text is the About Fake Company header, the intro paragraph, and the Fake's Beliefs section.

First of all, highlight the text you want to adjust. Then click on the Enlarge Text button (shown in Figure 11.7) to make the image bigger.

FIGURE 11.7
The Enlarge Text button.

Now that the text is larger, you need to adjust the font and color by taking the highlighted text and changing the formatting. The formatting section of Nvu appears in Figure 11.8.

FIGURE 11.8 *The formatting section of Nvu.*

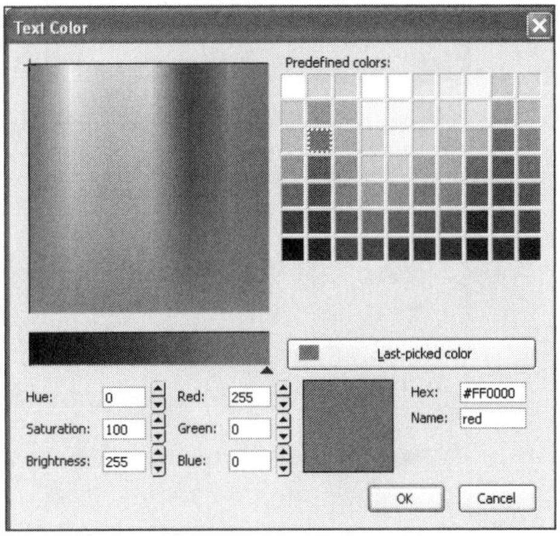

Click on the font selection box for a list of all the available fonts on your machine. Choose the best font for your page, but make sure it's common enough to be on every visitor's machine. Chapter 12 will go over font selection, but for this document, stick with Arial.

To change the color, you need to click on the color selector directly to the right of the font selection box. This makes the color wheel window pop up. This wheel is shown in Figure 11.9.

This color wheel allows you to choose any color in the spectrum. However, I recommend that you only use one of the predefined colors.

FIGURE 11.9 *The color wheel selector in Nvu.*

For the Fake Company Web site, let's use pure red. The color wheel selector should have a Red value of 255, and the Blue and Green values should both be 0.

Now the headers on your page should look like Figure 11.11. (This is WDFT11-04.html on the companion Web site.)

FIGURE 11.10 *Adding color to the page.*

WHY SHOULD I USE ONLY THE PREDEFINED COLORS?

When you open up the color wheel, you have a lot of colors from which to choose. A *lot*. However, I recommend that you stick to the predefined ones. There are a lot of reasons for this.

First of all, the predefined colors are the most common ones. Everyone recognizes the basic colors of red, black, green, and blue. However, people aren't used to seeing a green that has a hint of red and blue in it. Using predefined colors lets you have common and understandable colors on your pages.

The biggest reason, however, is compatibility. To check out how many colors you have on your computer, minimize all your windows, right-click on your desktop, click on Properties, and select the Settings tab (see Figure 11.11).

Look at your color quality setting. Does it say either Highest or Medium? If so, you can see most colors on your monitor. However, a lot of people have only 256 colors enabled. If you give them a color their monitors don't support, the color won't look right onscreen. This means that the page won't look how you want it to look. For this reason, you should stick to the predefined colors.

FIGURE 11.11 *The Settings tab.*

Pretty cool, huh? You've just added color to the page, and now the text is separated from the headers.

Why use headers at all? They allow you to separate the text into sections so that the visitor can figure out what he's reading. It's not just a continuous column of text. Breaking up text is incredibly important. Just as this book has numerous headers to break it up into sections, your Web page needs sections to help the visitor understand your message.

Finally, let's look at the code that makes up this page:

```
<html>
<head>
  <meta content="text/html; charset=ISO-8859-1"
 http-equiv="content-type">
  <title>Navigation Bar</title>
</head>
<body>
<table style="width: 100%; text-align: left;" border="0" cellpadding="0"
 cellspacing="0">
  <tbody>
    <tr>
      <td style="width: 10%;"><img alt="Fake Logo"
title="The FakeSite Logo" src="images/logocroppedcircle.gif"> </td>
      <td style="width: 5%;"><br>
      </td>
      <td style="width: 1px;"><a href="index.html"><img
alt="Visit the Index" title="Visit the Index" src="images/home.gif"
style="border: 0px solid ; width: 115px; height: 18px;"></a><br></td>
      <td style="width: 1px;"><a href="catalog/catalog.html"><img
alt="Catalog" title="Catalog" src="images/catalog.gif"
style="border: 0px solid ; width: 115px; height: 18px;"></a><br>
      </td>
      <td style="white-space: nowrap; width: 1px;"><a
href="about/about.html"><img alt="About Us" title="About Us"
src="images/about.gif"
style="border: 0px solid ; width: 115px; height: 18px;"></a><br>
      </td>
      <td style="white-space: nowrap; width: 75%;"><a
href="contact/contact.html"><img alt="Contact Uscontact/"
title="Contact Us" src="images/contact.gif"
style="border: 0px solid ; width: 127px; height: 18px;"></a><br>
      </td>
      <td style="vertical-align: top;"><br>
      </td>
    </tr>
  </tbody>
```

```
</table>
<br>
<table style="width: 100%; text-align: left;" border="0" cellpadding="2"
 cellspacing="2">
  <tbody>
    <tr>
      <td style="width: 50px; vertical-align: top;"><br>
      </td>
      <td style="vertical-align: top;"><big
 style="color: rgb(255, 0, 0);"><span style="font-family: Arial;">About
Fake Company</span></big><br>
      <br>
Fake Company was formed in 2004, the brainchild of John Fake. He truly
enjoyed allowing people to experience Fake stuff, so he created this company
to provide Fake goods to the public.<br>
      <br style="color: rgb(255, 0, 0);">
      <big><span style="font-family: Arial; color: rgb(255, 0, 0);">Fake's
Beliefs:</span><br style="font-family: Arial;">
      </big>
      <ul>
        <li>There should be Fake for everyone.</li>
        <li>Everything Fake is beautiful.</li>
        <li>There should be a worldwide understanding of Fake.</li>
      </ul>
      </td>
    </tr>
  </tbody>
</table>
</body>
</html>
```

Make sure that you look at how Nvu uses color. It adds color using style sheets with RGB values. It gives the red, green, and blue hex values in the code. Another way you could've adjusted the color would have been to use the COLOR attribute in the <FONT></FONT> tag.

Let's talk about using Fireworks to make cool header images.

Creating a Header with Fireworks

Macromedia Fireworks includes a lot of easy ways to make some really cool header images. A header image is like what you saw in Figure 11.1. It's a title bar that gives the name of the site.

First things first, you need to open up a new document in Fireworks. You want to make the header image big enough to have a large text layer; you can always scale it down later. Your New Document dialog should look like Figure 11.12.

The pixels per inch setting tells the resolution of the image. The more pixels per inch, the better the quality of the image, but also a larger file size. Usually, you'll want to stick with 72 pixels per inch or less because monitors can't display more than that anyway.

FIGURE 11.12 *Creating a new document in Fireworks.*

Now, you're going to convert that blank page into an awesome header image. Let's start off by adding text to the document.

To add text, select the text tool from the tool selector on the left. Look down at your text properties palette, which looks like Figure 11.13.

You want to make the header image very large, because it's at the top of the page. Choose 64 for the font size. You can make it larger or smaller if you want, but you don't want it to be too small to see or so large that it's annoying.

Also, make the font Arial Black. (I'm an Arial type of guy. I just like the font.)

FIGURE 11.13 *The text properties palette.*

DOES IT MATTER WHICH FONT I USE FOR A HEADER IMAGE?

The short answer: yes and no. That doesn't help much, eh? Well, there's a fundamental difference between using fonts on a Web page and using fonts in an image. On a Web page, the font is loaded from the visitor's computer. If the visitor doesn't have that font installed on his machine, the font won't look like it should.

However, with a header image, the font is part of the image, so it's never loaded from the visitor's computer. You don't need to worry if that particular font is installed.

All this means is that you can use any font you want in your header images, and it won't look any different to the visitor. This doesn't mean that you *should* use any font you want, though. Some fonts are ugly, and others are hard to read. Stick to fonts that are legible and pretty, and you should be okay.

After you've adjusted the font properties, it's time to make the text appear on the screen. Click somewhere in the document and type the title that you want to use. In this case, it's "Fake Company." The result is shown in Figure 11.14.

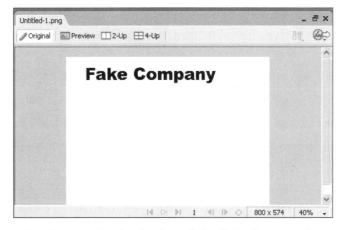

FIGURE 11.14 *The beginning of the Fake Company logo.*

note If you start the text too far to the right or left, some of the header image may go off the screen. To get it back onscreen, just select the black arrow tool in the tool panel and drag the header image. If your image doesn't fit at all, you need to resize the canvas by going to Modify > Canvas > Canvas Size.

Okay, now let's edit the header image. The easiest way to make it look cool is with Firework's built-in effects. Select the text and look at the tool properties palette. On the right side of the palette is the effects section, shown in Figure 11.15.

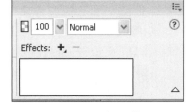

FIGURE 11.15 *The effects section of the text properties palette.*

Click on the plus sign to add effects. There are a lot of effects, so you should experiment with them to see what they do. For this chapter, you're going to use some of the more obvious effects.

The first effect you're going to use is Emboss, in the Bevel and Emboss section. Click on the plus sign and a panel pops up with options including Bevel and Emboss. Choose the Bevel and Emboss menu, and then choose Inner Bevel. The resulting header image looks like Figure 11.16.

FIGURE 11.16 *The effect of beveling on the text.*

So what just happened? Well, Fireworks added a cool shading effect to make the text look like it has depth. This stands out a lot more than flat text.

You can adjust the properties of the effect as well. Double-click on the effect in the Effects window. This brings up a number of options that you can use to adjust the effect (see Figure 11.17).

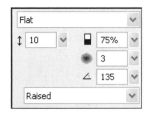

FIGURE 11.17 *The effect options.*

Pretty cool, huh? Hover your mouse cursor over one of these options, and a ToolTip pops up to tell you what the option does.

Okay, now let's add another effect. This effect gives a real feeling of depth because it creates a shadow on the page.

Add a new effect, and choose the Shadow and Glow item. Click on Drop Shadow. The drop shadow makes the header image jump off the page, as shown in Figure 11.18.

FIGURE 11.18 *A drop shadow under the Fake Company logo.*

The options for the drop shadow are pretty cool. One of the nicest ones is the direction of the shadow. You can change the location of the shadow so it looks like the light is coming from another direction. For example, in Figure 11.19, the drop shadow is going in the opposite direction from the one in Figure 11.18.

FIGURE 11.19 *Changing the direction of the drop shadow.*

Pretty cool, huh? The header image looks totally different.

Okay, that's enough about editing the header image. Now you need to crop it. Cropping removes everything from the header image but the part you want to keep. Do this by highlighting the header image and choosing Edit > Crop Image. Then you need to export it by going to File > Export Preview. A window pops up that looks like Figure 11.20.

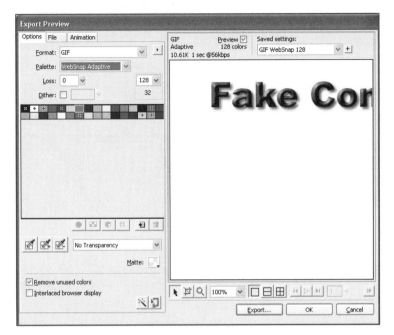

FIGURE 11.20 *The Export Preview window.*

Export it as an Adaptive GIF because of the file size and quality of the header image. Then you're asked to save the file to a location. Choose the Fake Company Web site directory in the images folder and click Save. By the way, it's a good idea not to put any spaces in the filenames of your images. Just like in HTML pages, having spaces in the filenames makes it difficult for some browsers to reference them correctly.

Now you need to add the header image to the About Us page. You want to add the header image above the road logo, indented to halfway across the logo. This can be done with another alignment table. Make sure you use pixels instead of a percentage, though, because you want it to be exactly halfway across the logo no matter which browser or screen resolution is used.

Let's do this in Nvu. First of all, you need to create an alignment table. You could create one from scratch, or you can just copy and paste the one you used earlier in the chapter. To copy the last table, click inside it, right-click, and choose Table Select > Table. Then select Edit > Copy from the menu bar at the top of the screen. Your selected and copied table should look like the one in Figure 11.21.

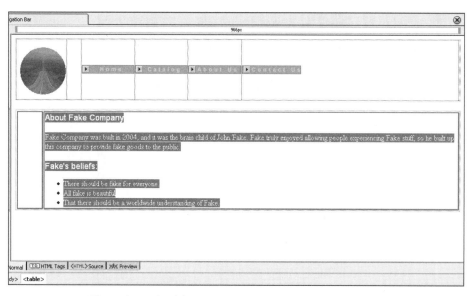

FIGURE 11.21 *The selected table.*

Now move the cursor above the road logo. Choose Edit > Paste, and your copied table appears. Just remove the text from the second column, and your window should look like the one in Figure 11.22.

Now you need to realign the table. The road logo is 108 pixels wide, so the alignment column should be one-half of that, or 54 pixels wide. Adjust this by right-clicking in the left cell and choosing Table Cell Properties. Change the width to 54, and the table will be aligned properly.

All you have to do now is insert the header image. This is as simple as clicking on the image button on the main toolbar. The Image Properties window pops up, as shown in Figure 11.23. Make sure you choose a local version of the header image so that you can reference it when it's on the Web.

Now the header image should look right. You've completely designed the page so it has a header image. Pretty cool, huh?

The final page looks like Figure 11.24.

By the way, the file is WDFT11-05.html as well as index.html in the About folder. The index.html file is the one you'll be using for the final version of the site, because it's properly located within its own folder. Take a few moments to look at the final code on the companion Web site. I'll wait here . . .

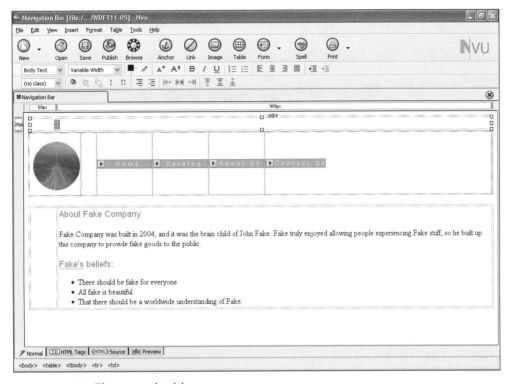

FIGURE 11.22 *The pasted table.*

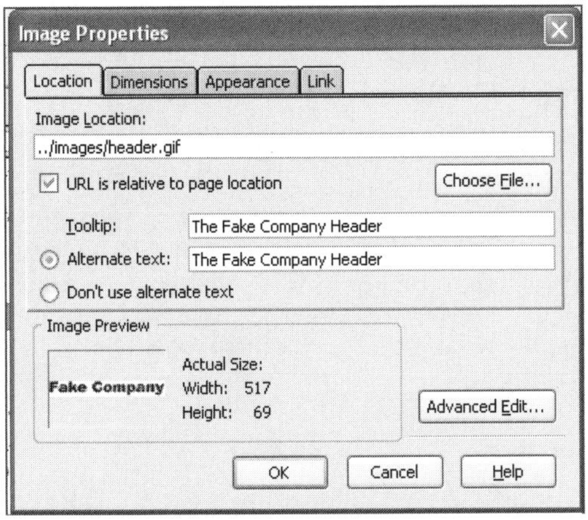

Image Properties

Location | Dimensions | Appearance | Link

Image Location:
../images/header.gif

☑ URL is relative to page location   Choose File...

Tooltip: The Fake Company Header

◉ Alternate text: The Fake Company Header

◯ Don't use alternate text

Image Preview

Fake Company Actual Size:
Width: 517
Height: 69   Advanced Edit...

OK Cancel Help

FIGURE 11.23 *Referencing the header image.*

FIGURE 11.24 *The final page.*

Sure, the code's a little long, but it's for the main page of the Web site. Most of the other pages will use the same code, with only small changes to adjust for each page's differences.

That's it for this chapter. One more and you're done with Part 3!

Summary

In this chapter, you learned a lot about using text in Web pages:

- ❖ Spacing and fonts
- ❖ Colors
- ❖ Changing colors and fonts in Nvu
- ❖ Making header images in Fireworks

I hope you enjoyed this chapter. Get ready for the next chapter, where you'll learn how to keep your source and files clean, as well as how to maintain compatibility with all browsers and computers.

Chapter 12

Compatibility and Cleanliness Issues

Hey, welcome to Chapter 12. This chapter is going to be a little short, but it's extremely important because it's about compatibility and issues with file and source cleanliness. These may not be the most fun issues to deal with when you're creating a Web site, but they're important nonetheless. Without compatibility, no one else can understand or even see your Web site. Without cleanliness, well, even *you* won't be able to understand it. Let's get to work.

Compatibility

So what is compatibility? Well, Dictionary.com defines it as "capable of orderly, efficient integration and operation with other elements in a system with no modification or conversion required." That's a little hard to understand, eh?

Compatibility is a lot simpler than Dictionary.com makes it out to be. It just means that the page looks the same to everyone else as it does to you. You want your page to be compatible with all browsers. You don't want to use obscure fonts that won't work on everyone's machines.

Compatibility

This means that something is "capable of orderly, efficient integration and operation with other elements in a system with no modification or conversion required." Or rather, that it works the same with everyone's machine.

So how do you achieve compatibility? You simply design for the lowest common denominator (LCD). The oldest, most obsolete machine out there should be able to view your site with no problems.

Right now, Internet Explorer is the most common browser, with Mozilla in second place. You should test your site on both browsers to make sure it looks the way you want it to. In addition, test it on different operating systems, such as Windows XP, Windows 98, Mac OSX, and Linux.

The most common screen resolution is 1024x768. However, 35% of computers still use 800x600 resolution. Designing for the LCD means making sure that computers using 800x600 can view the site with no problems.

Let's go over how to make sites compatible.

Making Sites Compatible

Browser compatibility is a big deal. Let me tell you a story:

For the last few chapters, we've been developing a Web site for a fake company called, well, Fake Company. As I was preparing the example site for this book, there was an error in the pages that I didn't catch. One of the items on the navigation bar was aligned differently than the rest. However, this error didn't appear in Mozilla Firefox, which is the browser I use most of the time. Figure 12.1 shows what the page looked like in Firefox.

FIGURE 12.1 *The About Us page in Mozilla Firefox.*

It did appear in Internet Explorer, unfortunately. Figure 12.2 shows the page in Internet Explorer.

When someone visits your site for the first time and sees a misshapen navigation bar, he may not like it. It looks ugly and out of place, and you definitely don't want to draw the visitor's attention to an error on the page.

So what is my point? I never would have caught this problem if I hadn't tested the site in both Firefox and Internet Explorer. It probably wouldn't have been a good omen to write a book about Web design and have a huge error in the example site!

After I tested the site in Internet Explorer and found the problem, what did I do? I fixed it! The error was simply a <BR> line that appeared in the other navigation items but not the Home item. Fixing it was a snap.

Testing your Web site in more than one browser is very important. Fortunately, it isn't very difficult. For example, let's say you use Internet Explorer and you want to test your page in Mozilla Firefox.

FIGURE 12.2 *The bad About Us page in Internet Explorer.*

First of all, make sure your page works perfectly in IE. There really isn't any reason to test the page in other browsers if it doesn't work in your own, right?

After that, install Firefox if you haven't already. It's available on www.maneeshsethi.com or www.mozilla.org. (I'll try to keep the newest version on my site.)

After installing the browser, just open up the page in it. In Mozilla Firefox, you can just select File > Open File and load the Web page (see Figure 12.3). A window pops up that lets you select the file. Just navigate to the page you're testing and check if it looks the same in Firefox as it does in Internet Explorer.

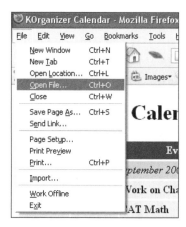

FIGURE 12.3 *Loading a file in Firefox.*

Resolution Compatibility

So now you know all about browser compatibility. But what about resolution compatibility?

There are a variety of screen resolutions, but the most common are 800x600, 1280x1024, and especially 1024x768. You need to test each page with different screen resolutions. Fortunately, it's very simple to check different resolutions on one machine. We've gone over it before, but let's do it once more.

Navigate to your desktop and right-click on the desktop area. You'll see the menu shown in Figure 12.4.

Select Properties. Choose the Settings tab, and you should see something that looks like Figure 12.5. Adjust the Screen Resolution option. It's as simple as that!

So what *is* resolution anyway? Resolution is the width and height of the visitor's monitor. This is measured in pixels, and it can be changed manually. If you make your resolution smaller, you're simply enlarging the pixels on your monitor so that you have fewer total pixels. This means less of the screen is viewable.

FIGURE 12.4 *Desktop properties.*

FIGURE 12.5 *Adjusting the resolution.*

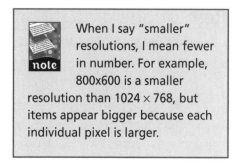

When I say "smaller" resolutions, I mean fewer in number. For example, 800x600 is a smaller resolution than 1024×768, but items appear bigger because each individual pixel is larger.

At smaller resolutions, Web browsers can show much less of the screen than at larger resolutions. For example, look at Figures 12.6, 12.7, and 12.8, which show the Fake Company site at three different resolutions.

FIGURE 12.6 *The Fake Company site at 800×600.*

FIGURE 12.7 *The Fake Company site at 1024 × 768.*

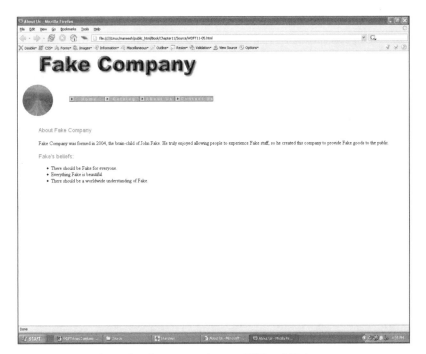

FIGURE 12.8 *The Fake Company site at 1280 × 1024.*

With this page, the different screen resolutions don't make too much of a difference. However, look again at Figure 12.6. Notice how there's a scroll bar on the right? That means the visitor needs to scroll down to see some of the page.

Not everybody likes to scroll down a page. There's a statistic that 50% of newspaper readers will only see the top half of the front page of the newspaper, simply because they're too lazy to open it up. This statistic remains true for Web sites—a lot of visitors won't look at anything past the top half of your page.

What does this mean to you? If at all possible, scale down your page so it can be viewed on 800 × 600 screens. More than 35% of computers use 800 × 600. You really don't want to annoy more than 1/3rd of your visitors, do you?

Scaling down your Web site isn't too difficult. You just need to resize your tables to make the page smaller. For example, if you want to make the About Us page smaller, just make the company header at the top smaller and scale down the road logo. Suddenly, the page takes up a lot less space.

There are a few more aspects of compatibility we could cover, mostly involving operating systems and JavaScript. However, most operating systems display Web sites in the same way, and almost all browsers these days have JavaScript enabled, so it isn't too big of a hassle.

There *is* one thing you should do, though. Always, and I do mean always, use the ALT attribute with the <IMG> tag to describe an image. Some visually impaired people have browsers that read the text on the page to them out loud. If your images don't have the ALT attribute, these people won't be able to hear the descriptions.

Also, some people still use text-only browsers, myself included. For example, Figure 12.9 shows what maneeshsethi.com looks like in the Lynx text browser.

Without ALT tags, text browsers cannot understand images at all. The ALT attributes give some context to the images on the screen. Unfortunately, some sites don't have the ALT attribute, which means that the images can't be understood in a text browser like Lynx.

Now you know a lot about compatibility. Make sure you keep your sites compatible with all browsers, resolutions, and everything else!

 **Maxim # 10**
"Always use ALT Tags, unless you don't want everybody to view your site."

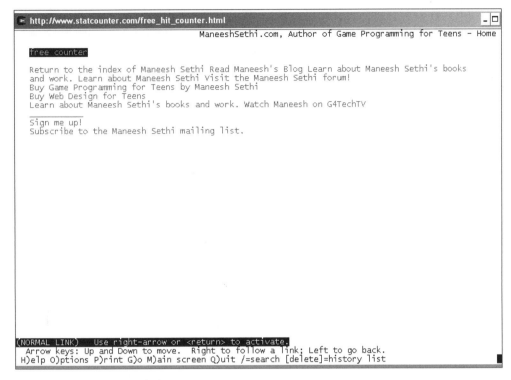

```
http://www.statcounter.com/free_hit_counter.html                        - □
                        ManeeshSethi.com, Author of Game Programming for Teens - Home
 free counter
 Return to the index of Maneesh Sethi Read Maneesh's Blog Learn about Maneesh Sethi's books
 and work. Learn about Maneesh Sethi Visit the Maneesh Sethi forum!
 Buy Game Programming for Teens by Maneesh Sethi
 Buy Web Design for Teens
 Learn about Maneesh Sethi's books and work. Watch Maneesh on G4TechTV
 _____
 Sign me up!
 Subscribe to the Maneesh Sethi mailing list.














(NORMAL LINK)    Use right-arrow or <return> to activate.
 Arrow keys: Up and Down to move.  Right to follow a link; Left to go back.
 H)elp O)ptions P)rint G)o M)ain screen Q)uit /=search [delete]=history list
```

FIGURE 12.9 *A text-only browser.*

Let's move on to the file structure of Web sites, which is very important to putting a Web site on the Internet.

File Structure

We went over file structure a little at the beginning of Part 3, but now that you've finished the site, it's time to go into more depth. File structure involves the locations of all of your files in relation to each other.

Because you link to other pages on your site using the `<A HREF></A>` tag, you need to know where all those files are located in relation to each other. You don't want to dump all the files in the same directory, though, because that directory will get crowded and you won't be able to understand the structure of your own Web site.

For this reason, you should add different folders to your site. Each folder contains the information for an individual page, so that the pages are broken up and the structure is easy to understand.

Take a look at Figure 12.10, which shows the file structure for the Fake Company site.

As you can see, there are four folders: about, contact, catalog, and images. The about, contact, and catalog folders contain information about those individual pages. The images folder holds the images for all of the pages.

Also, in the main folder there's a file called index.html. This is the home page, which looks like Figure 12.11.

So why name this file index.html? When Web browsers go to a site like www.something.com, first they look for a page named either index.html or home.html. I like to stick with index, because it's the most common name. The Web browser will show index.html usually by default, depending on the Web site's setting. If there's no index.html, either it returns an error or it shows all of the files in the directory, depending on the Web site.

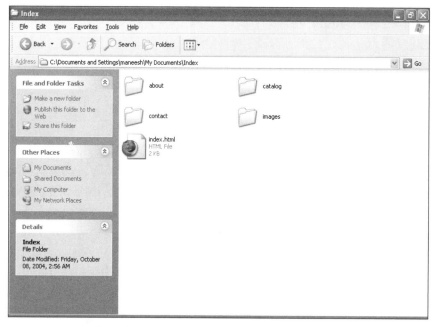

FIGURE 12.10 *The Fake Company file structure.*

FIGURE 12.11 *The Fake Company home page.*

Within each subfolder, the name of the page is the name of the file. That means when you go to the about folder, there's a file named about.html file in there. In the contact folder, the page is contact.html, and in the catalog folder, the page is catalog.html.

If you decide to use subfolders, you may want to name each individual page, index.html. If you choose to do this, then visitors who visit your page don't have to expressly type in the file name, because index.html will load automatically. For example, if you have a file located in the contact folder named index.html, you can get to that page by going to www.yoursite.com/contact.

The one problem is that if you set up subfolders like this, the image and link references may get messed up. The image link from the home page will be different than the image links from any page in any of the subfolders. For example, the reference to the header image on the home page may look like this:

```
<IMG SRC="images/header.gif">
```

However, the reference will be different for the About Us page, because it's in a different location with respect to the images folder:

```
<IMG SRC="../images/header.gif">
```

So what's the difference? For the About Us page, there are two periods before the images folder reference. These two periods mean that the Web browser first moves back one folder, going from the about folder to the main folder. Then it moves to the images folder, and then it references header.gif.

In all cases, including page links, you use two periods to move backward through the folder. These periods make the Web browser go backward so that you can locally reference any of the files you want.

You may be wondering why you can't simply use a global link, like this:

```
<IMG SRC="C:\Website\images\header.gif">
```

There are a lot of things wrong with this. Certainly, the page will look good on *your* computer, assuming the main page is located in C:\Website. However, when you put the page online, the links won't work at all, because there's no such thing as C:\Website online.

Let's say you have a Web site called www.something.com, and you refer to the header image as follows:

```
<IMG SRC="http://www.something.com/images/header.gif">
```

The image works correctly. However, this isn't a smart method of referencing images. A Web browser has a cache where images are loaded so they don't need to be reloaded the next time the visitor comes back. This makes the page load faster, because the browser doesn't need to load the same image over and over again. Unfortunately, when you use absolute links such as `http://www.something.com/images/header.gif`, the cache is cleared every time, and your pages will take much longer to load.

Instead, stick with relative links. They're faster, and they're also modular. You can take the file structure of your site and move it somewhere else, and the page will still work.

So now you understand that the linking structure will be different between the home page and the subpages. Let's take a look at the difference between the navigation bar on the About Us page and the one on the home page.

The following is the code for the navigation bar on the home page:

```html
<table style="text-align: left" border="0" cellpadding="0"
 cellspacing="0" width="511">
  <tbody>
    <tr>
      <td width="109"><img alt="Fake Logo"
title="The FakeSite Logo" src="images/logocroppedcircle.gif"> </td>
      <td width="40">    <br>
      </td>
      <td width="116"><a href="index.html"><img
alt="Visit the Index" title="Visit the Index" src="images/home.gif"
style="border: 0px solid ; width: 115px; height: 18px;"></a><br>
      </td>
      <td width="116"><a href="catalog/catalog.html"><img
alt="Catalog" title="Catalog" src="images/catalog.gif"
style="border: 0px solid ; width: 115px; height: 18px;"></a><br>
      </td>
      <td style="white-space: nowrap" width="116"><a
href="about/about.html"><img alt="About Us" title="About Us"
src="images/about.gif"
style="border: 0px solid ; width: 115px; height: 18px;"></a><br>
      </td>
      <td style="white-space: nowrap" width="127"><a
href="contact/contact.html"><img alt="Contact Uscontact/"
title="Contact Us" src="images/contact.gif"
style="border: 0px solid ; width: 127px; height: 18px;"></a><br>
      </td>
      <td style="vertical-align: top" width="1"><br>
      </td>
    </tr>
  </tbody>
</table>
```

Notice how each link refers directly to the image and page folders. That means the link to the catalog page is `catalog/catalog.html`.

Now look at the code for the navigation bar on the About Us page:

```
<table style="width: 100%; text-align: left;" border="0" cellpadding="0"
 cellspacing="0">
  <tbody>
    <tr>
      <td style="width: 10%;"><img alt="Fake Logo"
 title="The FakeSite Logo" src="../images/logocroppedcircle.gif" width="108"
height="126"> </td>
      <td style="width: 5%;"><br>
      </td>
      <td style="width: 1px;"><a href="index.html"><img
 alt="Visit the Index" title="Visit the Index" src="../images/home.gif"
 style="border: 0px solid ; width: 115px; height: 18px;" width="115"
height="18"><br>
        </a> </td>
      <td style="width: 1px;"><a href="catalog/catalog.html"><img
 alt="Catalog" title="Catalog" src="../images/catalog.gif"
 style="border: 0px solid ; width: 115px; height: 18px;" width="115"
height="18"></a><br>
      </td>
      <td style="white-space: nowrap; width: 1px;"><a
 href="about/about.html"><img alt="About Us" title="About Us"
 src="../images/about.gif"
 style="border: 0px solid ; width: 115px; height: 18px;" width="115"
height="18"></a><br>
      </td>
      <td style="white-space: nowrap; width: 75%;"><a
 href="contact/contact.html"><img alt="Contact Uscontact/"
 title="Contact Us" src="../images/contact.gif"
 style="border: 0px solid ; width: 127px; height: 18px;" width="127"
height="18"></a><br>
      </td>
      <td style="vertical-align: top;"><br>
      </td>
    </tr>
  </tbody>
</table>
```

See the difference? The reference to the Catalog page is now ../catalog/cata-
log.html.

Now you know a little bit about file structure. I recommend that you keep a folder for all the images, because you'll want to keep them all together. That way, if you want to change the images for all of your pages at once, you only need to make one change.

That's it for file structure!

A Quick Refresher: Code Cleanliness

I know we haven't talked about it for a while, but I want you to remember this: *It's very important to have clean, understandable HTML*. It should be tabbed and readable source that other people can understand.

A lot of people start relying on programs such as Nvu to do their coding, and they completely forget about coding by hand. Unfortunately, Nvu and other programs can lead to ugly source code. For example, Figure 12.12 shows the source code that Nvu displays for the home page.

Now that's hard to read! The tabs aren't correct, and some of the code branches out to multiple lines. When the code is converted into the HTML document, the source is cleaned up a little, but it still doesn't look as good as it can.

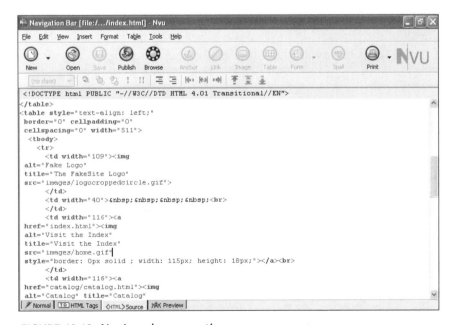

FIGURE 12.12 *Nvu's code generation.*

When you finish writing a page, either by hand or through a program, make sure you take a look at the source and see if anybody else will be able to understand it. If not, reorganize it!

Sometimes I take the Nvu code and capitalize the tags, just so they stand out against the rest of the code. This makes reading the code much easier.

Also, if there's a difficult section of code, I add comments by using the <!-- and --> tags:

```
<!-- The following section loads images into the document. -->
<IMG SRC="image.gif">
<IMG SRC="image2.gif">
<!-- End of image loading section. -->
```

You see how that works? The text inside the comment indicators isn't read by the browser, but other people can open up the source and read your comments.

Now you understand code cleanliness. That's it for Part 3! You're just about done with the book. Now all that's left is learning how to publish your site on the Internet, and how to make some money from it!

Note that this site isn't complete yet. The main page is very boring, and you haven't even designed the contact and catalog pages. I want to make this a contest: Redesign the site and make it the coolest you possibly can. Make sure you include all of the pages. E-mail your site to me at maneesh@maneeshsethi.com, and I'll display it on my site, maneeshsethi.com, so people can see your creation! Some of the best ones will win prizes such as free books and software.

Summary

That's it for Part 3. You've learned all about designing and developing a site. This chapter went over a bunch of important Web site design stuff that you should know:

- ❖ Compatibility between different machines
- ❖ File structure
- ❖ The importance of clean code

You're done with the design of the Web site. Next up, you'll learn how to put your site on the Internet! And don't forget about the contest. Redesign the site and submit it to maneeshsethi.com.

PART 4

WEB
DESIGN

for teens

Everything Else

In this final part, we will discuss what you can do with your Web site once it is finished. In the first chapter, you will learn how to get your Web site online. We will discuss buying a domain name, procuring hosting, and getting your Web site so that others can see it.

In the final chapter, you will learn how to drive traffic to your site. You will learn how search engines work, as well as how you can get others to link to your site. This part will be concluded by the heartfelt book summary, and an explanation of the contest in this book in which you can win prizes.

Chapter 13
Going Online

Welcome to Part 4! This part is a lot different than the rest of the book, because you already know how to make a full Web page. This part goes over how to go from an offline Web site to an online Web site. You'll put the Fake Company site online for all to see!

Here's the bad part about going online: It isn't free. You can make all the Web sites you want on your own computer for free, but publishing it for the whole world to see takes a little bit of money.

Of course, there are methods of getting a free Web site. You can submit your site to some places like www.angelfire.com or www.geocities.com, but the problem is that you don't get your own location on the Web. You will have a Web site that looks something like http://angelfire.com/mynamehere, and it just isn't as nice as having your own page.

You can check out these sites if you want, but we won't be going over them in depth in the book.

Fortunately, I did all of the scouting for you. I'm going to tell you about the hosting companies I use so that you can get the same good deal I get. Some hosting companies can cost between $30 and $50 a month. I'll teach you how to get online for a lot less.

There are two parts to getting online: getting a domain name and finding a host. Let's start off with getting a domain name.

Getting Named

Domain names are strange things, because they're simply a way for other people to remember your site. All domain names point to an IP address, such as 14.25.243.22. But what's easier to remember, cnn.com or 64.236.16.84? You can verify that this number takes you to the CNN site by typing http://64.236.16.84 into your Web browser and seeing what pops up.

 Accessing a page by typing in its IP address usually works, but not always. Some Web hosting companies block attempts to use IP addresses to access a page. maneeshsethi.com is one of these.

So what's the point of a domain name? It's just easier to remember than an IP number.

I'm sure by now you want to get your own domain name. How do you go about doing that?

 **Domain Name**

This is a string of characters that's separated by periods, used to access a Web page.

There used to be only one company that sold domain names, Network Solutions, and it only offered .com, .net, and .org domains. But today, many companies are in the business of selling domain names.

The cool thing about this is the competition—more companies means lower prices. Before, domains were always 25 bucks a year. Now, you can get them for no more than $10.

I've used multiple domain services over the past few years, and my favorite by far is Go Daddy at godaddy.com (see Figure 13.1).

As you can see, the price is a lot cheaper than $25. It's only $8.95 for basic domain name service per year. That's less than 75 cents a month!

So what does this get you? You get a domain name, such as yourname.com. People will be able to type in this domain name and go to your site. Pretty cool, eh?

The first thing you need to do is come up with a domain name that fits your site. For my personal page, I used maneeshsethi.com because that's my name.

FIGURE 13.1 *Go Daddy's site.*

For my previous book, *Game Programming for Teens* (it's a best-seller at Barnes & Noble, and you can find information on it at maneeshsethi.com), I called the site blitzprogramming.com because the book used Blitz Basic. You should pick a domain name that tells people something about your site.

I recommend that you pick a very simple name that is easy to remember. A lot of times, people will forget about hyphens, or they won't remember clever spellings, so try to use easy to remember names.

Unfortunately, only one person can own a domain name. If someone already owns a domain name you want, you're out of luck. Let's see if you can register fakecompany.com at Go Daddy. Type "fakecompany" into the domain name field and choose .com, just like in Figure 13.2.

FIGURE 13.2 *Testing out a domain name.*

Unfortunately, you get an error like the one in Figure 13.3. The domain name has been registered already, which means you can't use it.

That stinks, huh? No big deal, though. There are two ways to get around this situation. The first thing you can do is come up with a better name for your site. Maybe companythatisfake.com? No, that's really annoying. How about ourfakecompany.com? No, that still doesn't work very well.

You need to associate the URL with Fake Company, but without using fakecompany.com. Fortunately, by using the second way, you can use other suffixes for domain names these days. No one has taken fakecompany.org or fakecompany.net. Also, you can register fakecompany.biz, fakecompany.us, fakecompany.info, and lots more. The following list shows all of the different suffixes that Go Daddy offers:

❖ .com	❖ .info	❖ .ws
❖ .us	❖ .net	❖ .name
❖ .biz	❖ .org	❖ .tv

These are the most common suffixes on Go Daddy. There are some more, and you can see them by visiting godaddy.com.

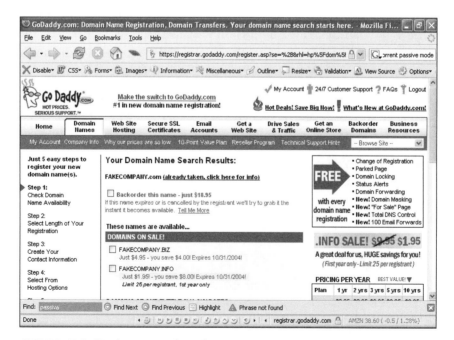

FIGURE 13.3 *Testing out a domain name.*

There is a problem with using suffixes other than .com. People remember .com a lot more than any other suffixes. Take for example, Dick Cheney, the Vice President. During a debate, he referred viewers to the site FactCheck.com. He actually meant to send to them to FactCheck.org, and FactCheck.com redirected visitors to a site that stated reasons why voters shouldn't vote for President Bush and Vice President Cheney!

There are a lot more available suffixes, but they're mostly reserved for different countries. Most domain names use .com, .net, or .org, but you can use any of these other ones if necessary.

Pretty cool, huh? For Fake Company, the .net suffix seems the best choice. Let's register it. Simply choose .net in the text box on godaddy.com. Figure 13.4 shows what happens.

It works! Fakecompany.net is a valid domain name.

Now you just need to register it. Click the Smart Registration button to get started.

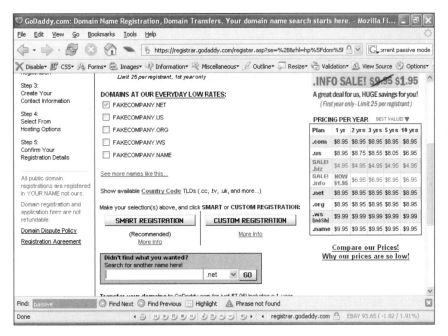

FIGURE 13.4 *Testing out a domain name.*

There are three steps to the registration process. The first step is to choose how long you want to own the domain (see Figure 13.5). If you're sure you're going to use this name, register for at least two years. If you aren't sure, just do it for one year.

You need to enter your name and mailing address at the bottom of this section. Then you're done with the first step. The next two steps are shown in Figure 13.6.

These are even easier than the first step. In step 2, simply choose whether your listing is standard or private. I recommend that you use standard, but read Go Daddy for more about the differences between standard and private listings.

At the bottom of step 2, choose whether or not you want to renew the domain automatically. If you don't, your domain will disappear after one year unless you renew it manually. This can be bad, because someone else might register it. Then you'll lose the domain for a long time.

FIGURE 13.5 *The first step in registration.*

In step 3, you simply need to choose a few options. You can have Go Daddy host the site for you, or you can have them hold your page until you find a host. Choose the latter so that you can host the page on your own.

I recommend GoDaddy for the domain name, but there are better options for hosting. For this reason, I usually choose the park option so that they hold the Web site name until I get someone else to host it.

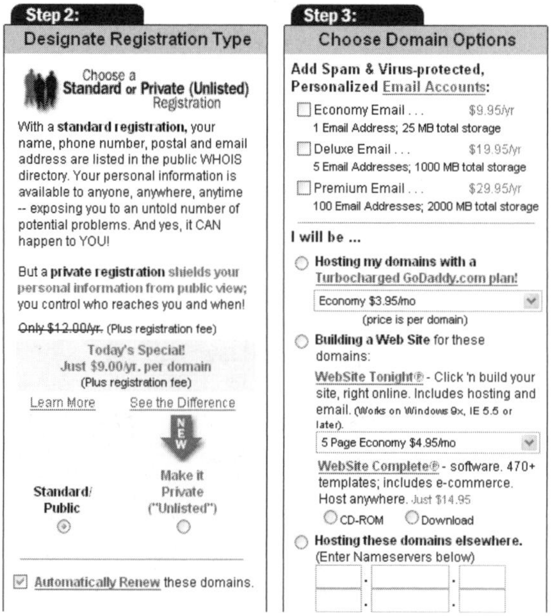

FIGURE 13.6 *The next two steps.*

After this, all you need to do is go through checkout, where you give then your credit card info and pay for the domain. It takes up to two days after payment before your domain name is available on the Web.

Hosting Your Web Site

You need hosting to actually make your site available on the Web. Without hosting, your site will never appear online.

You have a lot of hosting choices. Some of the best and most common hosting companies are expensive, nearly 30 bucks a month for the most basic service. Of course, you need to pay more for the cooler options. For example, if you want to have more than a gigabyte of space, you'll probably have to pay for it. However, you can usually find the basic services at cheaper prices.

I use two hosting sites, one for cheap hosting and one for more complex hosting. For complex hosting, I use word-associates.com because of all the features it offers, including Perl, PHP, CGI, and database support. Figure 13.7 shows everything that you get.

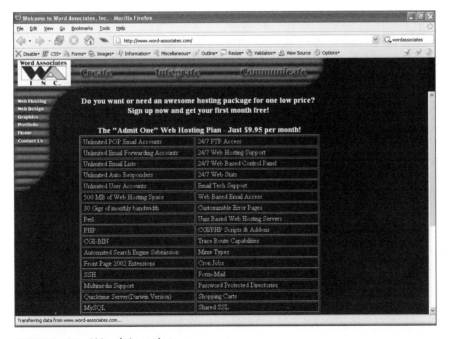

FIGURE 13.7 *Word Associates.*

Word Associates has a lot of features and a lot of memory. It also doesn't cost too much—just 10 bucks a month. (That's in addition to the price of registering the domain name.)

For cheaper and more basic hosting, I use E-RICE.net (see Figure 13.8). It's very good and very cheap. It doesn't accept as much usage, though, so it shouldn't be used for very popular or very large sites. Usage is the amount of traffic that your site gets, and the number of people that visit your site. For small sites, E-RICE should be just fine.

Hosting with E-RICE is really cheap. For about 10 bucks a *year*, you get 100MB of Web space and 10 e-mail accounts. That's an awesome deal. If you want more space, you can get the more expensive plans, which are only $10 or $20 more per year.

If you're not planning on using anything more complex on your site than HTML and maybe JavaScript, you can get a static account. This is a very basic

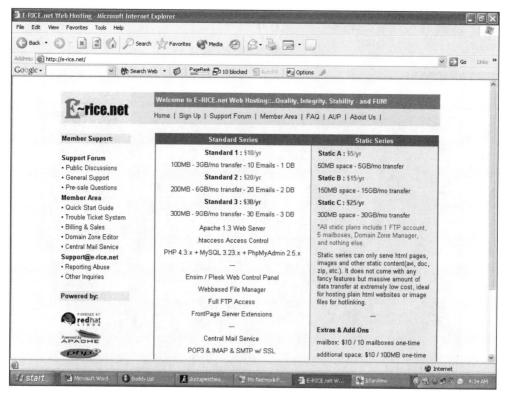

FIGURE 13.8 *http://E-RICE.net.*

account, because it only allows HTML. It's a really good deal if you've got a basic HTML site.

So let's say you choose the standard $10/year plan. The first thing you need to do is buy the plan. Click on Sign Up, and you'll see a page that looks like Figure 13.9.

In order to sign up for hosting, you need to have a domain name registered already. Choose a username and enter your domain name. You then need to pay by using PayPal, a service that allows you to send money over the Internet. You need a PayPal account to sign up for E-RICE, so go to paypal.com and follow the instructions.

What next? In a few hours, you'll receive a welcome e-mail that tells you to update your name servers. These are simply references by your domain name to your hosting service that allow them to be associated with one another.

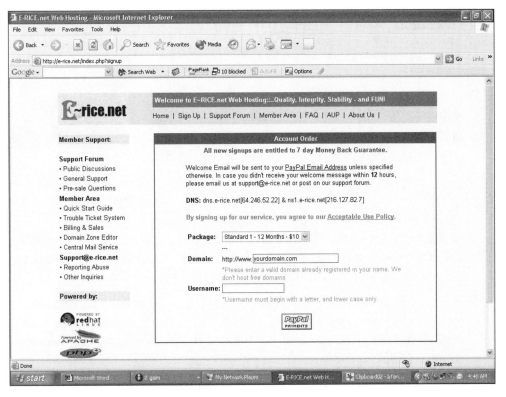

FIGURE 13.9 *Signing up for E-RICE.*

You need to go back to godaddy.com and log into your account to change the name servers. After you log in, choose the option to manage domains. The resulting navigation bar looks like Figure 13.10.

FIGURE 13.10 *Go Daddy's navigation bar.*

Click on Set Nameservers to go to the name servers page. You can then set the site's name servers, as directed in the e-mail sent to you by E-RICE. Most likely, your name servers will look something like the ones in Figure 13.11.

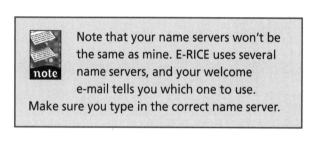

Note that your name servers won't be the same as mine. E-RICE uses several name servers, and your welcome e-mail tells you which one to use. Make sure you type in the correct name server.

FIGURE 13.11 *Setting up your name servers.*

Once you've set up the name servers, your page will be associated with your hosting service. Unfortunately, this takes two or three days. In this time, you can get your site ready to be uploaded to the Internet.

This waiting period is called propagation. It takes a couple of days before people around the globe can access your site because of all of the connections that need to be made, so you will probably have to wait a couple of days after changing the name servers to see the site.

Putting your site on the Internet is easy and free. All you need is an FTP program. One of my favorites, SmartFTP, is available on maneeshsethi.com. Install the program and run it, and you should see a window that looks like Figure 13.12.

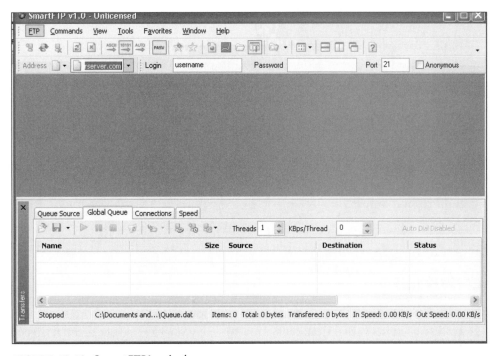

FIGURE 13.12 *SmartFTP's window.*

What is FTP? It stands for File Transfer Protocol, and it's a way to move files from your computer to the Internet. It's easy to do and doesn't take much time to learn.

FTP (File Transfer Protocol)
This is a method of transferring files from your home computer to your Web site on the Internet.

Pretty standard interface, huh? You need to enter three pieces of data to access your Web site—your Web site address, your username, and your password. Your Web site address will probably be ftp.yoursite.com, so if you bought johnsmith.com, type ftp.johnsmith.com into the Address box.

Next you need to type in your username. Typically, this is the same as the username you use for your hosting company. However, with E-RICE, your username is your e-mail address. For maneeshsethi.com, my username is maneesh@maneeshsethi.com. Check your welcome e-mail to see what you should type into the Username box while FTPing files.

Your password will be whatever you chose when you signed up for hosting.

After typing in this information, press Enter to log in to your account. To move files to the FTP server, you just need to open up the files in Windows Explorer and drag them into the FTP window. Make sure that you upload the files to your mainwebsite_html directory, or whatever your www directory is (your welcome e-mail should tell you).

After you transfer the files, they will appear in the window. After the domain name has been propagated (about two days after you enter the name servers), the files will appear on your Web site. From then on, uploads to the FTP site will happen automatically.

Congratulations, you've just put your Web site on the Internet!

Summary

That was fun, huh? You learned all about how to move files from your computer to an online server so that everyone can see your work. Specifically, this chapter taught you:

❖ How to get a domain name

❖ How to get hosting

❖ How to upload files to your Web site

Pretty cool, eh? You only have one more chapter! In the next chapter, you'll learn how to publicize your site and sell products and services on the Internet. Cool, huh?

Chapter 14
Getting Traffic

Welcome to the last chapter of the book. You're about to learn the art of attracting people to your Web site. You'll find out how to draw them to you, how to market your site, and even how to find out how many people are visiting.

Now get ready for some traffic!

Traffic

You need to get traffic to your site. *Traffic* just means how many visitors you have.

Getting people to come to your site is one of your most difficult tasks as a Web designer. Usually, the

Traffic

This is the amount of data that's transferred to and from your computer. In most cases, it's just a measurement of the number of people who have accessed your site in a certain period of time.

first step is to submit your site to search engines. Let's start off with Yahoo.com, which is second only to Google these days. Unlike Google, Yahoo allows you to suggest a site directly to their search engine. First, go to yahoo.com and scroll to the bottom of the page. You see a section that looks like Figure 14.1.

Click on How to Suggest a Site. On the resulting page, you can either pay to submit your site or not. Of course, paying will get you better results, but you probably want to do it for free.

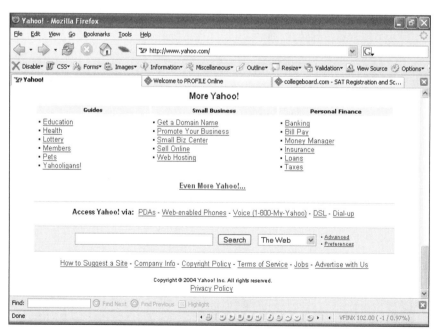

FIGURE 14.1 *Suggesting a site on Yahoo.com.*

The next page requires you to sign into Yahoo.com. If you don't have a Yahoo account, you can sign up for free. Then, just type your account information into the box and log in.

You're now at the first step to submitting your site. Your browser should look like Figure 14.2.

You need to type your URL into this box, including the www and the .com. Then wait until the next page is loaded. This is a confirmation page that says your URL is now on the list of sites Yahoo will crawl. In a few weeks, people can search for your site on Yahoo!

Now let's talk about what happens when you search for something on Yahoo. Let's say you own an Apple iPod and you're looking for an iPod case. Just go to Yahoo and search for "best iPod case." Figure 14.3 shows you the results.

What do you see? A bunch of results related to your query. And of course, the iPod case that I designed is #2 in the results.

So what just happened? The Web crawler crawled my page a few months ago, and it noticed a link to my iPod case. It then compared this link with links from

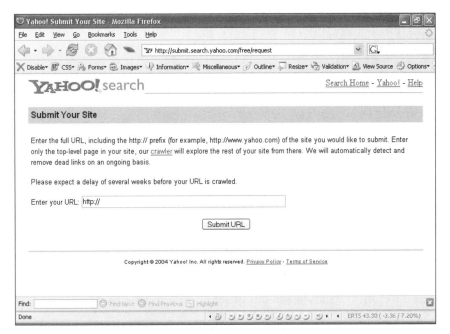

FIGURE 14.2 *The first step to submitting your site on Yahoo.*

FIGURE 14.3 *Searching for "best iPod case" on Yahoo.*

other sites, and it found that there were dozens of sites that were linking to my iPod case. Once it saw this, it recognized my site as a popular one and moved it to the top of the results page.

Google does the same thing, but without giving preference to sites that you submit. You can submit your site by going to http://www.google.com/addurl.html, but it probably won't appear very high on the results page. The submission page is shown in Figure 14.4.

So how does Google work if it doesn't give preference to pages that are submitted through its Add URL service? Google actually does something called *crawling the web*—sort of like what Yahoo did, but to a much larger degree.

Google starts with the base of pages that it's stored in its database, and then it follows all of the links attached to all of those pages. It records the number of times each individual link appears on the entire Internet, and the pages with the most links appear at the top of the results. This means that if you want your page to be popular, you need to get other people to link to it.

Let me tell you a story about traffic and page results. Remember that iPod case I told you about? I made it out of a sock. Figure 14.5 shows you what it looks like.

FIGURE 14.4 *Submitting your page to Google.*

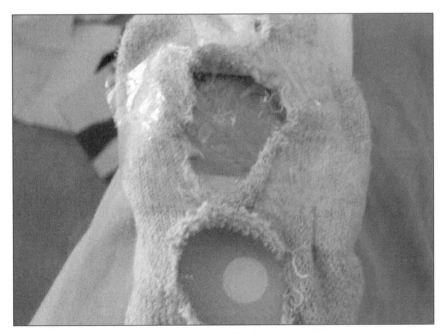

FIGURE 14.5 *My beautifully designed iPod SuperCase.*

Obviously, this was a pretty funny invention, so I put it up on eBay to sell it. At one point, the auction hit more than 100 bucks and got a lot of attention. Lots of really famous blogs (Web logs) around the country started posting links to it.

Google noticed these links and recorded them. Once it made a crawl through the Web and saw how many links I had, it shot my page to near the top of Google. Now I'm pretty high on the list if you search for "best iPod case" or "Maneesh."

So you probably want to get a lot of people to link to you. This can be relatively difficult, unless you have a product worth linking to. However, a lot of times you can make deals with other Web masters, where you link to their site and they link to yours. This is especially common with fan sites, like sites for videogames or card games.

To trade links with another Web master, you simply need to e-mail them. Go to other Web masters' sites, get their e-mail addresses, and ask if they want to trade links. Do it politely, and there's a good chance that they will. Once you get a lot of links, Google will recognize your page and shoot it to the top.

Another thing that Google checks is the number of times your page is updated. If you update it daily, you'll have a higher rating than sites that don't update as often.

Now that you know how to get traffic to your page, let's talk about how to find out how much traffic you're getting. This is done with the help of a nice little site called StatCounter.

Recording Traffic

There's a free service called StatCounter that records how much traffic your site is getting. This is invaluable when you want to know how well your marketing is working.

Go to statcounter.com. You will see a page that looks like the one in Figure 14.6.

The main page discusses all the awards and praise that StatCounter has received, and it's received a lot. It's an incredibly effective service.

You need to sign up for an account. Go to the Register section at the top of the main page. The Register page looks like Figure 14.7.

This page asks you to fill in some basic user information and agree to the terms and conditions. After you finish registering, you can log in to your account. From there, you can start tracking how many people are visiting your site.

FIGURE 14.6 *StatCounter.com.*

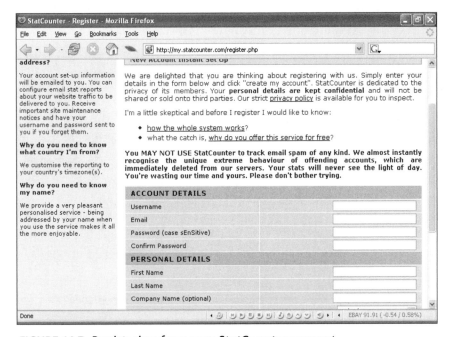

FIGURE 14.7 *Registering for a new StatCounter account.*

When you log in, it asks you to add a new project. This project is going to be your main page. StatCounter gives a long explanation about how their stats work, and you should read it. The most important thing is that StatCounter requires you to add some code to each of your pages. This code is then loaded every time someone visits your site, and your stats are updated accordingly.

Click on Add Standard StatCounter Project. The resulting page looks like Figure 14.8.

Not too hard, right? Just type in the basic information that's requested, and your project will be created. Also, you probably want to type in your own IP address (it's displayed for you) in the IP blocking section. Otherwise, you'll get counted for visiting your own page. That leads to faulty stats, so you probably want to stay away from that.

Now that you've created an account, you see a page that gives you more explanation on how to make this site work. The first thing you probably want to do is install your code. Click on the Install Code button to go to a page that looks like Figure 14.9.

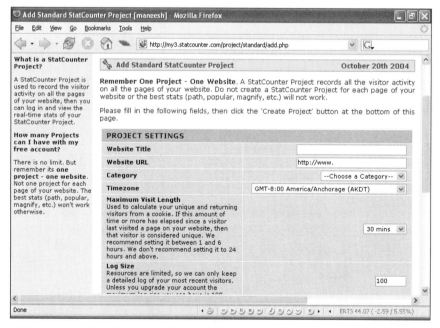

FIGURE 14.8 *Creating a StatCounter project.*

FIGURE 14.9 *The Install Code section.*

It's incredibly important that you follow these instructions. Otherwise the stats won't work, and in some cases your page won't look right.

As you scroll down, you see a text box that gives you the code you need to insert into all of your pages. It looks a little like the box in Figure 14.10.

The trick here is to put the code within the ⟨BODY⟩⟨/BODY⟩ tag, so it's somewhere in the main code section of your HTML document.

```
<!-- Start of StatCounter Code -->
<script type="text/javascript" language="javascript">
var sc_project=364123;
var sc_partition=1;
</script>

<script type="text/javascript" language="javascript"
src="http://www.statcounter.com/counter/counter.js"></script><no
href="http://www.statcounter.com/free_hit_counter.html"
target="_blank"><img
src="http://c2.statcounter.com/counter.php?sc_project=364123&am
alt="free hit counter" border="0"></a> </noscript>
<!-- End of StatCounter Code -->
```

FIGURE 14.10 *The code to be installed.*

So what do you do now? You open up all of the pages that you've created, and you add the code to them. Let's start off with the main Fake Company page. Open up the page in Notepad to view the source, and copy and paste the StatCounter code. The `<BODY></BODY>` section of the document should look a little like the following code snippet:

```
<body>

<!-- Start of StatCounter Code -->
<script type="text/javascript" language="javascript">
var sc_project=364123;
var sc_partition=1;
</script>

<script type="text/javascript" language="javascript"
src="http://www.statcounter.com/counter/counter.js"></script><noscript><a
href="http://www.statcounter.com/free_hit_counter.html" target="_blank"><img
src="http://c2.statcounter.com/counter.php?sc_project=364123&amp;amp;java=0"
alt="free hit counter" border="0"></a> </noscript>
<!-- End of StatCounter Code -->

<table style="width: 100%; text-align: left;" border="0" cellpadding="2"
 cellspacing="2">

<!-- …The Actual Page… -->

</table>
</body>
</html>
```

Not bad at all, huh? Note that there should be no changes to the actual layout of the page—everything should still look exactly the same. The page should look like Figure 14.11. (This is WDFT14-01.html on the companion Web site.)

You need to upload this page to your Web host again through FTP. (Chapter 13 explained how to upload files.)

Now it's time to check your stats! Go to StatCounter.com, log in, and click on the My Stats button for your project. If you've had a lot of visitors, you get a graph that looks something like Figure 14.12.

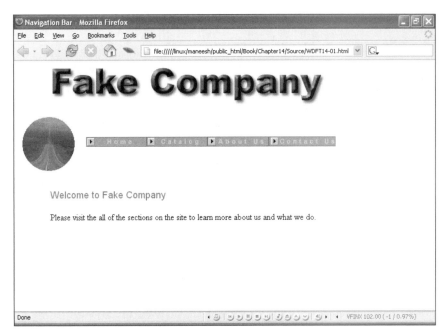

FIGURE 14.11 *The Fake Company page with StatCounter code added.*

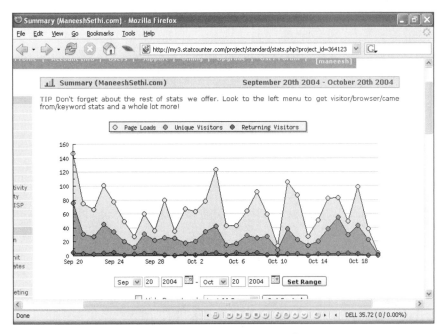

FIGURE 14.12 *The maneeshsethi.com visitor graph.*

This graph shows the daily activity on your site. If you scroll down, the data is listed for you.

The best parts of StatCounter are the links to the left of the graph. You have items ranging from entry pages to keyword analysis. The following is a list of everything you can access:

- ❖ Popular Pages
- ❖ Entry Pages
- ❖ Exit Pages
- ❖ Came From
- ❖ Keyword Analysis
- ❖ Visitor Paths
- ❖ Visit Lengths
- ❖ Returning Visits
- ❖ Recent Pageload Activity
- ❖ Recent Visitor Activity
- ❖ Country/State/City/ISP
- ❖ Browser
- ❖ System Stats

That's a lot of information! Each page contains a wealth of knowledge about those who've accessed your page. Figure 14.13 shows the System Stats Page.

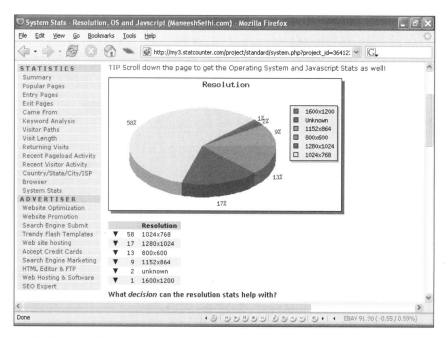

FIGURE 14.13 *The System Stats page.*

There's a lot more than resolution info here. Scroll down to learn about the visitors' operating systems and whether their browsers support JavaScript.

The coolest part about StatCounter is that you can get more information about individual people who've visited your site. This lets you learn more about each individual visitor. First you need to go to a section that lists the visitors. Try the Visit Length page, shown in Figure 14.14.

The bottom of the page shows you how many people have spent specific amounts of time on your site. Next to each measure of time is an arrow. Click on the arrow to get a list of information on individual visitors. The arrow does not give actual names of visitors, but it gives their IP address, their location, and some information about their system.

Click on a visitor you want to know more about, and you get a drill-down page that looks like Figure 14.15. Note that the visitor's IP address has been blacked out for security reasons.

Whoa! A map that lists the visitor's location and everything. Sweet!

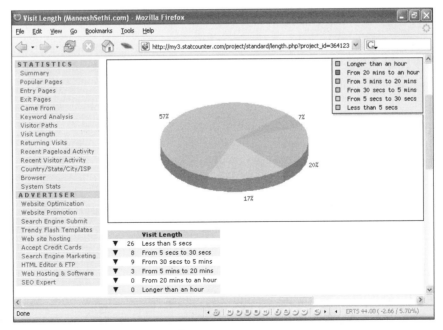

FIGURE 14.14 *The Visit Length page.*

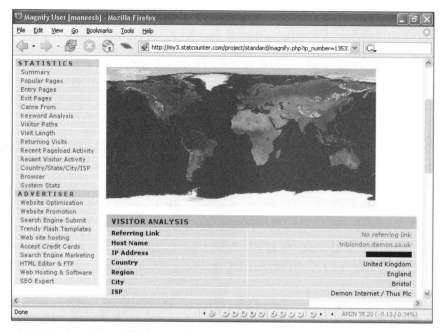

FIGURE 14.15 *The drill-down visitor analysis page.*

StatCounter offers a lot of possibilities, and it does the job very well. You can learn more about the people who are visiting your site, and you can use that info to make your site better.

Summary

The End. We're done. That's really it for this book. You sure learned a lot for such a small book, huh? You know everything you need to make a darn good site.

You started from scratch. You learned basic HTML. You learned more advanced HTML. Then you even learned how to apply it to specific concepts, such as navigation bars and individually designed Web pages.

It's amazing what a few hundred pages can do, huh?

I want you to keep working on Web design. Don't think of this book as the end of the line. There are lots of other things that you can do, such as Flash animation, JavaScript, PHP programming, and much more. Heck, I'd like to write a book on some advanced concepts someday. E-mail me with your requests! My e-mail address is maneesh@maneeshsethi.com.

Keep applying what you know, and someday you might be a masterful designer.

And don't forget the contest! If you can redesign the Fake Company site to make it prettier or better in any way, send it to me. If it's good, I'll post it online as part of a portfolio of people who've read my book. The best ones will get a reward! Go to http://www.maneeshsethi.com and click on the *Web Design for Teens* section. There's more info there.

If you liked this book, check out my others. I have written *Game Programming for Teens*, also published by CoursePTR, and this book can show you how to make great games of your own. Also, I am almost done writing *How to Succeed as a Lazy Student*, a book that will teach you all you need to know about surviving in middle school, high school, and college. Learn more about these at maneeshsethi.com.

Again, I want you to e-mail me! Just say hello, tell me if you liked the book, what my next one should be. Also, come to the maneeshsethi.com forum, where lots of Web designers just like you ask and answer questions. Come join the community.

I hope you've enjoyed this book. Keep working, and one day you'll be an awesome designer. And when you are, make sure you let me know!

By the way, if you want to keep up to date with the work that I'm doing, go to www.maneeshsethi.com/subscribe.html and type in your e-mail address. You won't get spammed, but you will get some cool information.

Lastly, for the first few people who ask, I'm willing to give you some free Web space. Just e-mail me, and I'll get you some free hosting so you can test out your page. All you have to do it visit my site or e-mail me. And while you're doing that, why not buy an iPod case? Just go to http://www.maneeshsethi.com/ipod.

> From this day to the ending of the world,
> But we in it shall be remember'd;
> We few, we happy few, we band of brothers;
> For he today that sheds his blood with me,
> Shall be my brother
>
> —William Shakespeare, *Henry V*

Appendix A
List of HTML Tags

T his section contains a list of all of the HTML tags we used in the book, in alphabetical order.

`<A> </A>`
This tag tells the browser that an anchor is occurring; that is, either a link or a named anchor.

`<B> </B>`
This tag makes the affected text bold and darker, see `<STRONG> </STRONG>`.

`<BGSOUND> </BGSOUND>`
This tag allows you to play background sound files in Internet Explorer.

`<BLOCKQUOTE> </BLOCKQUOTE>`
This tag sets a section of text away from the margins. You can nest these tags to indent even further.

`<BODY> </BODY>`
This tag encloses the entire actual text and code that appears on the screen in the HTML document.

`<BR>`
This tag adds a line break to the page

`<DD> </DD>`
This tag defines an item within a definition list.

`<DIV> </DIV>`
This tag allows you to align more than one paragraph at a time.

`<DL> </DL>`
This tag sets up a definition list.

\<DT\> \</DT\>

This tag creates an item that will be defined within a definition list.

\<EM\> \</EM\>

This tag makes the affected text italicized, or tilted slightly, see \<I\> \</I\>.

\<EMBED\> \</EMBED\>

This tag allows the embedding of other types of files directly into a page, including both sound and video.

\<FONT\> \</FONT\>

This tag allows you to adjust the font size, face, and color

\<FORM\> \</FORM\>

This tag tells the browser that a form is about to be created, and also explains what action the form will take.

\<HEAD\> \</HEAD\>

This tag contains information that is embedded in the page but does not actually appear on screen. The most important item in the header is the title, which appears on the browser icon.

\<HTML\> \</HTML\>

This tag encloses the entire HTML portion of your Web page; in most cases it is the first tag in the source.

\<I\> \</I\>

This tag makes the affected text italicized, or tilted slightly, see \<EM\>\</EM\>.

\<IMG\>

This tag tells the browser that there is an image to be displayed. The SRC attribute is required

\<INPUT\>

This tag tells the browser which control should be created within the form and what it should do.

\<LI\> \</LI\>

This tag defines the items within a list.

\<LINK\>

This tag allows you to add externally linked style sheets to your page.

\<OL\> \</OL\>

This tag sets up an ordered (numbered) list.

\<P\> \</P\>

This tag begins a new paragraph.

\<S\> \</S\>

This tag draws a strikethrough line through the affected text.

\<SPAN\> \</SPAN\>

This tag allows you to add style sheets to as much text as necessary.

\<STRONG\> \</STRONG\>

This tag makes the affected text bold and darker, see \<B\> \</B\>.

\<STYLE> \</STYLE>

This tag is used to define the style sheets for the entire Web page in the \<HEAD> section.

\<TABLE> \</TABLE>

This tag encloses the entire table and allows the browser to display the following row and column tags.

\<TD>

This tag creates a new data cell in a table.

\<TEXTAREA> \</TEXTAREA>

This tag creates an elongated text box that allows the user to enter in lengthy comments.

\<TH>

This tag creates a new header tag in a table.

\<TITLE> \</TITLE>

This tag defines the title of the page, and places that title in the name of the browser at the top of the screen and also in the system taskbar.

\<TR>

This tag creates a new row in a table.

\<U> \</U>

This tag underlines the affected text.

\<UL> \</UL>

This tag sets up an unordered (bullet point) list.

Appendix B

Glossary

This section contains a list of all of the definitions and maxims we covered in the book. First, the definitions.

Glossary of Definitions

Cascading Style Sheets

This is an extension to HTML that allows Web designers to specify styles such as font and color for specific elements on the Web page.

Comments

These are human language additions to an HTML document that are not read by the browser but aid in understanding what is occurring within the code. Comments are contained in between the symbols <!-- and -->.

Compatibility

This word means that something works the same with everyone's machine and browser.

Cropping

This is a way to get rid of all the unwanted information in an image. By using cropping, you keep the important part of the image and cut out the rest.

Domain Name

This is a string of characters that is separated by periods and gives a method of accessing a Web page. This points to a specific IP address or Web server where the site is hosted.

Filename Extension

The few letters that appear after the period in filenames, also called the suffix. For most Web sites, you will use the extension .htm or .html

Form

This is a set of controls placed on the page in which the user can enter information. Later, the form is sent to a server to be processed.

FTP (File Transfer Protocol)

This is a method of transferring files from your home computer to the computer that hosts your Web site.

Hexadecimal Notation

This is a way to define colors so that they can appear on the screen as a background, font, or horizontal line.

HTML (HyperText Markup Language)

This is the backbone code that goes into every Web page that makes text and graphics appear on the screen.

HTML Command

HTML code that is between '<' and '>' brackets. This information is read by the Web browser and influences the document, but does not appear in the document itself.

HTML Ending Command

HTML code that ends a previous command. It is signified by a '/' in front of a command name, for example, `</title>`.

Hyperlink

An object that allows you to move between pages in the Internet or to different points on the same page.

Image Format

A type of image that can be viewed on a Web page, typically GIF, BMP, PNG, or JPG.

Mystery Meat Navigation

This occurs when a user has to do extra work to find out where the navigation menu will take him.

Navigation

This is a method of allowing visitors to a Web site to move between pages. Without navigation, visitors will not be able to visit any other page except the home page.

Pure HTML Editor

This is the type of editor where you write and edit the HTML code directly.

Tag Attribute

This is an addition to an HTML tag that changes the action of the tag in some way.

Traffic

This is the amount of data that is transferred to and from your Web server. In most cases, it simply is a measurement for the number of people that have accessed your Web site in a period of time.

WYSIWYG (What You See Is What You Get)

This stands for the type of editor that allows you to see exactly what will appear on the screen as you edit the file.

Glossary of Maxims

Maxim #1
"The best design is one that the user doesn't even notice."

Maxim #2
"Never make the visitor work harder than he has too. Even better, never make the visitor work. Period."

Maxim #3
"Keep it Simple, Stupid."

Maxim #4
"Never, ever, use Mystery Meat Navigation."

Maxim #5
"Never use an obtrusive background. Make sure that if you do use an image, it is pleasing to the eye."

Maxim #6
"Don't overuse bolding, it won't help."

Maxim #7
"Be careful with multimedia. Especially when it is annoying."

Maxim #8
"Your images should always stand out. Not just against the background, but against the text, also."

Maxim #9
"The first color is white, the second color is black, and the third color is red."

Maxim #10
"Always use ALT tags, unless you want people not to view your site."

Appendix C

Guide to the Companion Web Sites

The companion Web sites to this book include the source and many useful programs to the book. There are two locations for the companion Web site: www.courseptr.com/downloads (the publisher's Web site) and www.maneeshsethi.com (my Web site).

The directory structure should be pretty easy to follow. You will find everything arranged like this:

Listings\

    Chapter01\

    Chapter02\

    ...

    Chapter14\

Programs\

Following is an explanation for all of these categories.

Listings

On each Web site, you will find all of the HTML code from the examples in the book. I recommend that you copy all of the samples to your hard drive so that you can play around with them. I will offer the source for each chapter in a single zip file so that you can download the entire source at once, or you can view each file individually.

Programs

This section contains a few programs that you can use in your conquest of the Web site designing world. You can download these demo programs directly from my Web site, www.maneeshsethi.com. The www.courseptr.com/downloads Web site will only include links to the programs' Web sites.

❖ **Macromedia Fireworks**—The image editor that we used to make navigation bars.

❖ **Jasc Paint Shop Pro**—An art program, much like Microsoft Paint, but much more robust.

❖ **Nvu**—Our HTML editor.

❖ **Mozilla Firefox**—The best browser out there.

Okay, that's about it for the Web site. Have fun with everything that is included!

Index

Symbols

A